FOUNDATIONS OF MODERN PSYCHOLOGY SERIES

Richard S. Lazarus, *Editor*

WILLIAM W. LAMBERT

Professor of Psychology, Sociology and Anthropology, Cornell University; researcher in social and experimental psychology, specializing in social learning, personality development, and cross-cultural research.

WALLACE E. LAMBERT

Professor of Psychology, McGill University; researcher in experimental and social psychology, specializing in the psyschology of thinking, language, and bilingualism.

Social

Psychology

PRENTICE-HALL, INC., *Englewood Cliffs, New Jersey*

IN MEMORY OF HARRY BROWN LAMBERT

SOCIAL PSYCHOLOGY, *William W. Lambert and Wallace E. Lambert*

PRENTICE-HALL FOUNDATIONS
OF MODERN PSYCHOLOGY SERIES
Richard S. Lazarus, *Editor*

PRENTICE-HALL INTERNATIONAL, INC., *London*
PRENTICE-HALL OF AUSTRALIA, PTY., LTD., *Sydney*
PRENTICE-HALL OF CANADA, LTD., *Toronto*
PRENTICE-HALL FRANCE, S.A.R.L., *Paris*
PRENTICE-HALL OF INDIA PRIVATE LIMITED, *New Delhi*
PRENTICE-HALL OF JAPAN, INC., *Tokyo*
PRENTICE-HALL DE MEXICO, S.A., *Mexico City*

Designed by Harry Rinehart

C–81806(p), C–81807(c)

Foundations
of Modern Psychology
Series

The tremendous growth and vitality of psychology and its increasing fusion with the social and biological sciences demand a new approach to teaching at the introductory level. The basic course, geared as it usually is to a single text that tries to skim everything—that sacrifices depth for superficial breadth—is no longer adequate. Psychology has become too diverse for any one man, or a few men, to write about with complete authority. The alternative, a book that ignores many essential areas in order to present more comprehensively and effectively a particular aspect or view of psychology, is also insufficient. For in this solution, many key areas are simply not communicated to the student at all.

The Foundations of Modern Psychology is a new and different approach to the introductory course. The instructor is offered a series of short volumes, each a self-contained book on the special issues, methods, and content of a basic topic by a noted authority who is actively contributing to that particular field. And taken together, the volumes cover the full scope of psychological thought, research, and application.

The result is a series that offers the advantage of tremendous flexibility and scope. The teacher can choose the subjects he wants to emphasize and present them in the order he desires. And without necessarily sacrificing breadth, he can provide the student with a much fuller treatment of individual areas at the introductory level than is normally possible. If he does not have time to include all the volumes in his course, he can recommend the omitted ones as outside reading, thus covering the full range of psychological topics.

Psychologists are becoming increasingly aware of the importance of reaching the introductory student with high-quality, well-written, and stimulating material, material that highlights the continuing and exciting search for new knowledge. The Foundations of Modern Psychology Series is our attempt to place in the hands of instructors the best textbook tools for this purpose.

Contents

Social Psychology, Its Major Concerns and Approaches

Social psychology is the experimental study of individuals in their social and cultural settings. Through training and experience, the social psychologist is encouraged to raise his sights from strictly psychological concerns and to include in his perspective the social world that affects the behavior of individuals and influences their modes of interacting. When a psychologist's perspective has been broadened to this extent, he comes to realize that psychological processes must be examined in the light of the many social influences that contribute to the development and ultimate style of human personalities. Because he is as interested

I

1

in social and cultural settings for behavior as in individuals, he conducts his experiments with both social context and individual in mind, controlling, where possible, the effect of one when he is concerned with the other.

Some of the social experiences in peoples' lives, however, are unique, tied to particular moments, whereas others recur again and again in much the same sequence or with much the same cause or effect. It is to these *recurring* processes that social psychologists turn, and it is largely with an eye to increasing our understanding of them that social psychologists experiment, construct theories, and develop methods of measurement. Consider, for example, two persons who are meeting for the first time, setting in motion the acquaintance process. Human beings have long been interested in this recurring social event and just recently Professor Theodore Newcomb at the University of Michigan conducted an extended experimental study of it.* Becoming acquainted is a far more complex process than we may at first think, as we shall see in Chapter 5. One of the reasons it is complex and difficult to observe is that it depends so much on what goes on within the two persons involved— the particular motives and wishes, the personality traits, attitudes and learnings from the past that they bring with them, and the accurate and inaccurate information they receive from and about one another. No one who wants to describe and experiment with the acquaintance process can ignore such inner states. In fact, the habits, attitudes, perceptions, judgments, and motivations of each participant make the acquaintance process possible and give it a particular style. At the same time, these personal factors are themselves modified through the process of social interaction. The social psychologist attempts to describe and explain both the psychological effects of social contact and the social process itself. For example, by standardizing the social context in which acquaintance takes place, he can explore individual differences in reacting to this form of social interaction, and by observing large numbers of unacquainted individuals in various social contexts, he can examine the general nature of the acquaintance process itself.

So social psychology leans on other branches of psychology. But this is not the end of the story because the concerns of social psychologists are of interest to all behavioral scientists, even to historians. Sociologists, for instance, have played a particularly active part in developing our discipline because recurring processes like becoming acquainted also depend on social rules and structures for their occurrence and facilitation. For instance, it is particularly rare and difficult for the low man in a social order to become acquainted with the top man. To study the social situation in detail, we must know about and be able to use the theories and measures provided by sociologists. Social psychology is indeed often referred to as "micro-sociology" or "micro-anthropology" since the analyst must lower his sights from the larger problems of these disciplines to see the finer texture of person-to-person

* T. M. Newcomb. *The acquaintance process.* New York: Holt, Rinehart and Winston, 1961. (Selected references are given so that the interested reader can turn to more extensive treatments of important topics.)

relationships—the converse of raising his sights from the usual concerns of psychology.

Social psychology is, then, a meeting place of many interests, ideas, and facts. In recent years, the discipline has grown greatly until now it is one of the lustiest children in the behavioral science family. It is a boastful and raucous child, possibly because it has so many parents. And it has its growing pains that sometimes result in a messiness and disarray of facts and theories. But one can view the disarray as a sign of creativity, and the boastfulness as a preliminary step to self-confidence. At any rate, we shall assume that this is the case in this book.

Many of the recurring processes that social psychologists have turned their attention to are the very ones that are supposedly already explained by common sense. When common-sense notions become part of one's everyday language, they are accepted by many as wisdom and are often used as principles for action or codes of conduct. Naive notions such as "Man is basically selfish" or "The more you get to know someone, the more you like him" are now challenged by social psychologists who ask these questions: "How do these codes work their way into the very structure of our language?" "To what extent do we act or judge on the basis of such notions?" "Are they valid?" It is at this point of challenge that the excitement of modern social psychology can be acutely felt, and it is largely in this century that the general critical tenor of Western thought has reached into the realm of social psychology with a serious intent to awaken us from our "dogmatic slumbers" regarding the social nature of man. Social psychology plays an important role in human affairs by developing methods and criteria for discovering what our common-sense—or even our more sophisticated—notions about interpersonal behavior actually are, and for checking their validity against standards more precise than whether they are charming or personally satisfying.

When we view the extreme variations in the interpretations of man's social nature that have appeared over the ages, we realize how great a need there is to check on their validity. Through the past centuries, man has been assumed, for example, to be perfectly rational, totally irrational; largely kind, rootedly cruel; especially aggressive, basically benign; a creature of wishful illusion, a purveyor of valid insight into the nature of things. What is intriguing about these doctrines is that each one was put forth by otherwise profound and reasonable people as a sufficient explanation of man's complex social nature. Apparently the social philosophers who proposed them were in search of what Gordon Allport of Harvard University has called "a simple and sovereign" doctrine on the social nature of man,* that is, a type of philosophical Ohm's law that would be as simple as possible but still explain as much as possible. These doctrines have left their mark on our everyday language and each has its ardent proponents today.

* G. W. Allport. The historical background of modern social psychology. In G. Lindzey (ed.). *Handbook of social psychology,* Cambridge: Addison-Wesley Co., 1954, Vol. 1.

Social psychologists, then, consider it their scientific business to challenge not only simple and sovereign doctrines but also more sophisticated ones, to construct fruitful ways of testing their validity, and to develop more comprehensive explanations of the social nature of man, explanations based on empirical facts. Because of their probing, it has become clear that simple and sovereign solutions are neither simple nor sovereign when carefully scrutinized. When someone argues that all social behavior stems from man's egoism, he appears to say something fundamental. He seems to be able to explain a great deal with this assertion, not only instances of selfish disregard for others but also cases where people help one another because, the argument goes, they receive a selfish feeling of satisfaction or some other benefits from helping. But, we ask, how can one distinguish between egoistic helping and egoistic hurting? People usually do want to make just such distinctions. The assertion can still remain tenable if the theorist shifts ground and explains that "helping someone is different from hurting someone because helping occurs when selfishness has been temporarily satisfied," or that "there is less selfishness in helping than in hurting."

In either case the doctrine is no longer simple. In the first, man's selfish nature has gained the property of a *state* of satisfaction; in the second, the notion of a *quantity* of selfishness has been added. When we reach this level of complexity, we are ready for some modern questions: Just how temporary is a "temporary satisfaction"? In what circumstances does it occur? How much difference in "selfishness" is there between "helping" and "hurting"? And, most important of all, by what means are we to measure the differences in the amounts of these quantities? When *these* questions are answered, the original formulation then becomes testable and the really interesting work of modern social psychology can commence.

There is no general agreement among modern social psychologists on approaches to the study of man's social nature. In fact, there are major differences in assumptions made about social behavior, in theoretical orientations to social-psychological problems, and in research strategies developed to examine these matters. We shall compare a few of the more important approaches now so that you will realize in the chapters to follow how much the types of research conducted and the conclusions drawn are determined by the theoretical assumptions made by a social psychologist as he plans his experiments. The differences of approach are interesting in themselves and are useful because they lead to theoretical arguments that in turn stimulate improvements in research.

One school of thought maintains that real progress will be made in understanding social behavior when social psychologists content themselves with describing the observable actions of people in various social contexts and refrain from theorizing about people's attitudes, feelings, or motives, that is, the nonobservable bases of behavior. There are many who find this approach congenial and they play essential roles in the development of modern social psychology by producing reliable facts about behavior that later become the cornerstones of good theories. When we look into the rudimentary forms of social interaction and the acquaintance process in Chapter 5, or the effect of groups on individual behavior in Chapter 6, we shall demonstrate how necessary it is to describe each stage in the development of interpersonal associations and each aspect of the social contexts in which interaction takes place.

Others argue, however, that such an approach is too inductive. It is primarily suited, they maintain, to the study of very simple forms of behavior, but not appropriate for the explanation of complex social behavior. This school of thought believes that social psychologists should deal squarely with the complexities—the motives, attitudes, values, perceptual styles of individuals, for example—and study how these personal dispositions develop, how they affect social behavior, and how they, in turn, are affected by social contacts. Although it seems straightforward enough, this theoretical approach is complex because it requires that the researcher concern himself with nonobservables. That is, he must create techniques for *inferring* the existence of attitudes or motives (neither of which can be directly observed) from careful observations of behavior in various social contexts. The task is much like the physicist's when he infers the existence of an atom from observing certain natural events that are presumed to depend on atomic activity. Neither attitudes nor atoms can be directly observed, but both can be indirectly measured. In fact, on the basis of such nonobservables, theories can be created that are as exciting and useful for social psychology as they are for the physical sciences. When we examine the development of motives and personality styles in Chapter 2 and the nature of social attitudes in Chapter 4, the potential value of this approach will become apparent.

There is one other important difference of viewpoint among contemporary social psychologists that will concern us. Some argue that too much attention in theory and research has been given to personality dispositions built up through long-term social experiences to the neglect of the relatively short-term field of forces—the events of the immediate social environment—that affect behavior quite independently of the past history of the persons involved. When a prisoner of war collaborates with his captors, it is asked, should we search for an explanation of his actions deep in his personality or in the immediate social setting where pressures are brought to bear on him? When people conform, is it because they have particular dispositions built up over the years that make them conformists, or would *anyone* conform if the circumstances are made just right? Those who emphasize the short-term influences provide us with basic principles that tell us, for example, how to put pressure on someone to change his behavior. They also show us what the limits of such pressures are and what social and cultural contexts they work best in.

Many social psychologists now see value in both these approaches and design their research so that it can reflect the joint effects of short- and long-term influences. This recent movement encourages researchers to look painstakingly into both the learning process that shapes personal dispositions and the various aspects of the immediate field of forces. We shall highlight this new movement as much as possible in the chapters to follow.

One of our purposes in this book is to communicate the conviction of social psychologists that, through careful study, man's social nature will be revealed and that as we begin to understand these complexities we also begin to understand ourselves. A second purpose is to communicate the fun and excitement enjoyed by social psychologists as their work progresses. Our chapters deal with some of the recurring processes of contemporary interest. But since these are terribly complex matters, we must keep our knowledge about them in perspective—we have made only a beginning, in some cases hardly even that. But the fun, excitement, and hopes of the disciplines can be clearly recognized in the beginnings themselves, even in the brief introduction to them we can present here.

In Chapter 2 we shall examine some of the ways that social influences leave their traces on individuals, especially young people who are being taught to be members of their societies. The focus of attention will be on the development of the child's conscience, his sense of identity, as well as the development of his dispositions toward aggressiveness, compliance, affiliation, and achievement. In other words, the emphasis will be placed on the broader categories of behavior that become integrated into distinctive personality styles. In Chapter 3, the focus is shifted to the adjustments people make to their social environments—how they come to perceive and judge people and events in shared ways and in individualized ways. In Chapter 4 we look further into the ways people cope with their environments as we study how people's thoughts, feelings, and tendencies to react become organized around certain recurring social events. These organized modes of thinking, feeling, and reacting are referred to as attitudes, and we shall describe how they function, how they are measured, how they affect behavior, how they develop, and how they can be modified. In Chapter 5 our focus alternates between the individual and the events that take place between two or more people as they interact. We try to explain how associations among people become established, develop, or disintegrate, and how those involved are affected by the interaction. The same theme is elaborated further in Chapter 6 as we describe the psychological consequences of belonging to groups and try to explain why some people adjust their behavior to the social demands of groups and why others take advantage of the opportunities available to them in groups to become leaders. In that chapter we also discuss how variations in the organization of groups affect the action of members, how pride in groups develops and sometimes leads to intergroup conflict, and how personal conflict can arise when one tries to belong to potentially antagonistic groups. In the final chapter our view of groups is broadened to include societies and cultures, thus permitting us to look into the role that these more extensive groups play in shaping man's social behavior and permitting us to touch on the large question of the causal relationships that exist between the processes of social psychology and those of the other behavioral sciences.

Socialization

Our personalities are shaped and developed in part through social contacts with other people. This process of socialization starts when we are infants and progresses, as we grow and learn, to the point where we come to behave, to think, to feel, and to evaluate things more or less as those around us do. An infant becomes a child whose behavior is similar in a great many ways to that of the other members of his family and social groups. Socialization continues, at a slower pace, all our lives. It may accelerate again when, say, a liberally educated college student, capable of a broad range of thinking and evaluating, enters a large

7

2

bureaucracy and gradually takes on the thoughts and judgments of the new particular community around him. What is the common theme in these examples? To a large extent, current researchers and theorists are concerned precisely with the problem of determining what the elements of the socialization process are and how they interrelate to give that process a general form. Although social psychologists have made progress in understanding certain of the parts, we are a long way from seeing the total outline and its limits.

Not that we lack assumptions and even theories about the total process, however. A comon notion, which describes what we have seen in the examples, is simply that an individual comes to be more and more like those who surround him. But this notion may be so limited that it leads to error, the error of watching *only* similarities—paying heed, for example, to the ways a minister's son comes to resemble his quiet and serene father, only later to discover that the boy has actually developed all the properties that make him a happy and successful sergeant in the Marines. Clearly, it would be unwise to prejudge socialization as a matter of increasing similarity of the neophyte to those that train him. For some of the most fascinating examples of socialization are the "failures"; the daughters who rebel and act exactly as their mothers would not, the professional soldier who retires and becomes a pacifist, the "well-trained" generation that leads a revolution against society and makes fundamental changes in it.

Of course, it is true that most societies continue in large part to rebeget their social kind from generation to generation, but the reasons why they can succeed in doing so are complex. Perhaps they perpetuate similarities by conscious teaching or training of the young, or by the relatively unthinking pressures they continually keep their members under from birth to death, or by their failure to provide more "satisfactory" alternatives.

Many of the problems of social psychology are clearly seen in the study of social pressures on personality development. That process has been of interest to social psychologists for two important reasons. First, knowing the conditions of personality development helps us to focus on the interpersonal, or social, processes and so improve our understanding of their relationship to adjustment, development, and learning. Second, personality development is itself the interpersonal process *par excellence,* since inevitably it occurs under the direction, or at least in the company, of others. Language and personal styles of speech, for example, can only be picked up from others, and language learning is typical of socialization as a whole.

RESOCIALIZATION

Perhaps we can get to the heart of some of the social psychological aspects of personality formation by first considering an attempt at personality destruction, the effort of the Chinese communists to *de*socialize American prisoners of war, to wipe out the effects of their previous socialization. We shall rely here on the report of Edgar Schein,* a social psychologist who interviewed many of the men on their release. The Chinese attempted not only to wipe out the socialization of the American soldiers but also to *re*socialize them, to make the Americans similar to themselves, particularly in political beliefs and values. But the Chinese failed in their basic aim. They did succeed in peripheral ways, and these frail successes give us insight into the juggernaut power of the usual massive socialization through which all human beings continually pass.

To desocialize a man to the point where he can be fundamentally changed requires a control of the great social structures that help keep him what he is. The United States Army, like all military bodies, is set up to turn a man into a courageous soldier (a socialization process in itself). The Chinese took officers away from their men, and with the officers went the constant rehearsal of learned roles that helps maintain army structure. They separated out the noncoms lest army structure and cohesion be reinvigorated at a lower level. They broke up companies and squads, to leave each man even more alone. They put minority-group members together so that lurking feelings of injustice could not be tempered by close companionships that might develop among captives of different backgrounds.

This policy left only the less tangible structures of informal social organization—the friendships that intertwine and overlap in a group and provide much of the social cement for day-to-day behavior. But the captors were highly inventive in breaking friend from friend and preventing acquaintanceships from forming so that men might find peace with one another. Weak men were lured by special treatment into informing on their comrades; their special treatment became clear enough to the other prisoners to be demoralizing. Yet they could never be certain whether other men were also hidden informers. To know and like another person, of course, requires trust—and the principal aim of the Chinese was to destroy trust. For without it, the main social controls on everyday behavior would disappear. At least, so went the theory.

The men, now isolated and alone, were then lured or forced to listen to constant and clever propaganda devised to teach them the bad side of what they had come from and the good aspect of what they would join if they would recant and take on the beliefs of their captors. But listening was not enough. The captives had to be induced to participate actively in their own retraining. Not all at once, however. Let them first develop the habit of confessing trivial wrongdoings, such as minor infractions of prison rules. Such confession, if rewarded, would possibly lead to a habit of public apology that might spread to other actions, to deeper beliefs.

To become like persons in control may depend on envying their power and privileges. And envy was easy for the Chinese captors to arrange. But they

* E. H. Schein. *Psychiatry,* 1956, 19, 149–172.

also had sense enough to know that they must themselves seem potentially likeable. Added to threats, then, were the lures that patience and kindness could provide, the rewards that accrued from collaboration.

In all, then, the men were made to feel alone, to be afraid; their minds were filled with constant propaganda, with both living proofs of the changes in fortune that a change in beliefs could bring about and with the terror that lay in resistance. We called it "brainwashing" and for a time saw in it something mysterious and frighteningly powerful. Now we know that we were seeing an everyday technique, but from a perspective that could give us insight into the technique's potential for taking away from human beings some of their hard-won identity.

But by and large the Chinese failed. They were dealing with mature men and these men were set against them. Some did break, but usually because of some insufficiencies in their background training. Some were bent, but straightened out when they returned to their usual world. Some rebelled and either died or endured great trouble. Most, though, used their wits, played it cool, and survived with a deepened insight into themselves and others. We do not know exactly why the Chinese failed, but their failure highlights the effectiveness and strength of the processes that had made these men into "Americans" and later into "American soldiers." They had human ties and ideas that were hard to eradicate, personal bonds that mass methods could not touch. They had traits, motives, and deep wishes that could only be satisfied back home. They could fall back on their wit and intelligence and the healing balm of hearing their own language with its dialects and intonations and all that it could remind them of. The Chinese were not attuned to all this, and their great effort could be frustrated by a Brooklyn-born soldier publicly reading a passage in Karl Marx with a humorous southern accent.

THE SOCIAL CONTEXT OF PERSONALITY FORMATION

Let us deal more intensively now with the social influences that help to form personalities and consider how vigorously community and family work on the biological material of their young members.

The Community

It is not difficult to document the influence of social contacts on the formation of personalities. At the very least, a child learns the names and some of the properties of a number of people, and begins to pick up knowledge of the multiplicity of "roles" these people assume. With some individuals, and even with some groups, he may develop deep ties that are highly influential in the formation of his habits of judgment and action. Such interaction is critical both as a direct influence on later actions and as a source of models for behavior.

Recently Roger G. Barker and Herbert F. Wright * have studied the public side of these formative influences, summarizing them neatly in terms of the number and kinds of *settings* in a child's life. Their core idea is that a growing child (or adult for that matter) is formed in part by his thousands of encounters with the tough and hard-to-change qualities of the public settings of his community. People, they point out, are more "docile" than the settings themselves. Thus, for a child who begins to ache from sitting on a church bench it is easier to move and wiggle than to change the seat, just as it is easier to go along with the traditional segregation of people expected in some settings than to change the setting itself.

Barker and Wright showed that it is possible to count all the public settings in a town and to treat each one as a scientific unit for social psychological study. Once all the settings are isolated and described, they can be compared for similarity, so that only those that are distinctive in some way are retained as worthy units for study. Thus, some settings Barker and Wright originally considered were not sufficiently distinctive to be retained as separate settings for study—"the entrance to the drug store" and "the introductory speech at the local lodge" were not kept as different settings from "the drug store" and "the lodge meetings," whereas it was useful to differentiate "the Baptist Church" and "the most popular local swimming place."

Barker † selected all the reasonably distinct settings in an American town and in a larger but generally comparable English town. The American town yielded 579 public settings for its 715 inhabitants; the English town had only 494 settings for its 1300 inhabitants; the ratios were 1.18 per person in "Midwest, U.S.A." and .55 per person in "Yoredale, England." These differences cast light on some of the sources of the differences in American and English character. Let us look at the children. In Midwest the average child fills 8.4 responsible positions in his community, in Yoredale only 2.7. Midwest adolescents play 16.6 responsible roles, English adolescents only 4.7. This difference continues into adulthood and old age. There are simply more settings in the American town, and the people are called on to fill roles in more of them. Children are less segregated in the American town, also: 52 per cent of all settings are open to them, whereas their English counterparts are excluded from 77 per cent of their town's settings.

It is from such social contexts that character is formed, argues Barker, pointing out that a primary psychological fact about the ecological environment of behavior in America has not been abundance of resources, but rather scarcity of people for the country's behavior settings.

Although the resistant behavior settings may alter in time, the softer stuff of which the human actors are made changes as a result of the environ-

* R. G. Barker and H. F. Wright. *Midwest and its children.* Evanston, Ill.: Row, Peterson & Co., 1954.

† R. G. Barker in M. R. Jones (ed.). *The Nebraska symposium on motivation, 1960.* Lincoln: University of Nebraska Press, 1960.

ment. One of the "principles of settings" (if Barker is correct) is that each one calls for an optimal number of participants and if there are too few participants then those few will be more pressed, and pressed in more varied directions. Such is the difference between Midwest and Yoredale, and it is in Midwest that we might hear an adolescent told: "You may not know much about acting, but we have to find someone to play Hamlet!"

The American children, then, participate more intensively in more settings than do their English cousins. One important phase of future research may be the investigation of the results of these social conditions. Can it be that because of such greater pressure American character *is* what we sometimes think it is: active, resourceful, sociable, hopeful, and a bit anxious? Or does the existence of such a national character lead to the formation of such a great number of settings in the first place? Will American character change with an increase in population and with the continued movement from small towns to urban centers and back out to the suburbs?

At any rate we have the beginning of a method for studying the potential influence of the qualities of settings on the malleable properties of the people in them.

The Family

Of all formative influences on socialization, the family, which provides the nonpublic settings in a child's life, has received the most intensive study. Psychologists have been evolving theories about, and methods to study, this area in recent years, and as a result are beginning to put together potentially far-reaching knowledge. Here we see at its full complexity the recurrent problem of social psychology—that of isolating data for study—since in addition to socialization the internal psychological processes of both parent and child and the rapid, constant changes in the child as a result of physical maturation are factors to contend with in the family in particular. In many studies this problem has received little or no attention, and in many others it has been insufficiently dealt with. It is fortunate that a new growth of interest in research on both animals and human beings has fostered the joint study of genetic factors and maturational stages *together with* the influence of social and other environmental differences.

Our focus here is on differences among families and general social environments, and probably the most informative route to the heart of the matter lies in tracking the principal ways family pressures on a child differ from family to family and from society to society.

A study recently carried out by teams of researchers from Cornell, Harvard, and Yale,* sought the important dimensions of difference in small communities in six different cultures: North India, Okinawa, Mexico, Africa, the

* B. Whiting (ed.). Six cultures, studies of child rearing. New York: Wiley, 1963; and W. W. Lambert and L. Triandis. *J. abnorm. soc. Psychol.,* 1961, Vol. 62, No. 3, 631–639.

Philippines, and the northeastern U.S.A. A group of children was studied in each community and the youngsters' mothers were kind enough to give long interviews on how they and other family members dealt with the children, thereby providing a great deal of raw data on the differences in pressures the children meet. These data were then reduced, with the help of the statistical technique of factor analysis and the use of a modern computing machine, to seven major independent types of differences (listed below). It turned out that all these differences in family pressures are due preponderantly to differences among mothers rather than among cultures; indeed, a number of them are found in studies dealing only with America.

Family settings differ greatly, then, in the following ways: (1) the demands for responsibility made on children, that is, the number and kinds of duties expected of them; (2) the emotionally positive behaviors of mothers to their children, such as praise, absence of physical punishment, and general warmth; (3) the degree of control demanded over aggression toward peers both inside and outside the family; (4) the degree of control over aggression and disobedience toward parents; (5) the extent to which the mother does the caretaking of babies; (6) the extent of her caretaking of older children; (7) the degree of the mother's emotional stability (does she blow hot and cold?).

This is not an exhaustive list—an exhaustive list will not be possible without far more research carried out in many more cultures—but it does provide a tool for comparing private settings, and it increases our realization of the immense and powerful differences we must consider in constructing theoretical models of the processes of socialization and personality development. As we shall see below, some of these differences have already been uncovered in research into specific facets of socialization.

SOME STRANDS OF THE SOCIALIZATION PROCESS

Socialization starts when new-born children, complete with all their various (and largely unknown) genetic differences and their potential for rapid maturational changes, enter a world in which the above-mentioned pressures from others begin to work on them in both public and private settings. Let us look at the developmental history of some of the strands of this process that psychologists have managed to describe fairly adequately. Besides trying to unravel some of those threads, we shall begin to search for apparent common principles. Afterwards we shall attempt to see the process in its larger outlines.

Social Compliance

The Fels Institute at Antioch, Ohio, which is justly famous for devising strategies of research on socialization, has recently focused * on the conditions under which children

* V. J. Crandall, S. Orleans, A. Preston, and A. Rabson. *Child Development,* 1958, 29, 429–444.

come to comply with the commands and suggestions of other people. The strategy here calls for tapping the home pressures related to the fourth factor (control of aggression and disobedience) discovered in the six-culture study mentioned above. It also calls for observing children of different ages at home and at school and for setting their compliance tendencies in the context of their total behavior.

The Fels researchers discovered that compliance tendencies begin rather diffusely but become more consistent as a result of what happens to a growing child. Thus, it is not possible to predict whether a young (three- to five-year-old) child will be compliant or resistant at school from a knowledge of his parents' policies of reward and punishment. But it is possible to make predictions on the basis of this knowledge for older children, and (as is often found with other strands of socialization) rewards appear to be more effective in inducing compliance than do punishments.

As children become older, their behavior becomes increasingly consistent. At the nursery-school age, children are somewhat uniform in complying with adults both at home and at school, but are not so with peers. Consistency in compliance with both peers and adults is high with older (six-, seven-, and eight-year-old) children.

In relation to children's over-all behavior, compliance takes a shift from the early to later years. In nursery school, a child who is compliant with his peers tends also to be generally dependent on them for physical help, emotional support, and approval. At the same time, however, he tends to act aggressively or hostilely towards them. In contrast, the child who is compliant only with adults, and is ready to withdraw from adult company and do things on his own, is marked by low aggressiveness and dominance. In short, when a child is young, dependency is related to compliance with peers but it is not related to compliance with adults.

It appears further that adjustment to adults is a basic factor in the older child's adjustment. Among the six- to eight-year-olds, help-seeking and dependency no longer distinguish the children who are compliant with peers, and those who are compliant with adults are no longer markedly self-reliant. What is left is a consistent difference in dominance and aggressiveness, the compliant children exhibiting less of each than the noncompliant youngsters. Each child now behaves much the same way toward peers as toward adults, at home and at school. Public and private pressures, and his own maturation, have resulted in a clear and consistent pattern by the time a child is eight—he has become either a dominant or a submissive person. But these traits seem to have nothing to do any longer with sociability or independence. Socialization and maturation have led to more consistent behavior with regard to compliance, but compliance no longer seems related to other traits as before.

This strand of socialization, social compliance, apparently involves a long sequence of learning. Children learn habits of compliance in interaction with their parents, forming them in response to the kinds of rewards and punishments the parents use or to the models of behavior they present. This habituated behavior is generalized early to other adults who supervise them in nursery school, and it eventually comes to characterize even behavior with peers. We might say that compliant behavior is a special case of instrumental learning (the process whereby habits are shaped by the temporal relation of their occurrence with respect to rewards and punishments) and that this process is managed by various important other people, prominent among whom are the parents.

Let us leave our interpretation for a moment and note some more general points: First, we have not discovered whether these American children are more or less compliant (or dominating and aggressive) than children from other cultures—that would require a more complex research plan. Nor have we ruled out the possibility that compliance or dominance may be due to gene structures. Heredity may determine the direction of a child's development, or it may cause a child to behave in such a manner that his parents feel called upon (for their own comfort or because of their sensitivity to social norms) to attempt to manipulate his development through rewards or punishments. To discount this possibility would require more knowledge of genetic matters than we now have.

Nor have we ruled out other explanations. Those familiar with Freudian language may suggest that the growth of such behavioral consistency from nursery school to grade school occurred as the child "internalized" parental values in coming to identify with the opposite-sex parent (thus resolving the Oedipus or Electra complex). Others would point to the greater consistency of parental pressures toward older children and claim that their more consistent behavior merely reflected this new home pressure, as well as the increasing pressure in the older children's public settings toward playing roles calling for consistent dominance (leaders) or consistent compliance (followers). Thus, children's behavior would shift as they grew older in response to the direction of these immediate pressures. Plainly, available interpretations of the socialization process are numerous and rich.

Despite the technical and theoretical issues raised, the study we have been discussing points up some clear relationships that help us to see the developmental history of compliance among some American children. A start has been made here, and the variety of possible interpretations with regard both to the facts and the theories of compliance need not confuse us—they will either lead to studies that add to the picture or they will not. In science the fruitfulness of research developing from a theory is more consequential than the brilliance of argument at any point.

Aggressiveness

We have already mentioned that aggressiveness tends to be low when compliance is strong. This may be of only incidental interest in the study of compliance, but since all cultures attempt to control aggressiveness, it often takes the center of the stage. The development of aggressiveness seems to have a more complicated history than does compliance; perhaps, though, we merely know more about it. Most psychological matters turn out to have complex compositions once we begin to study them.

A good deal of interest in aggression was stimulated by the development of a specific principle of behavior relating frustration and aggression by Leonard Doob * and his colleagues. This notion is that some form of frustration precedes aggressive behavior, but that frustrations do not always lead to aggression (though they *tend* to) since other behavior (such as compliance) may conflict or interfere with its expression. Research on the implications of this notion has shown it to be useful. But the frustration-aggression hypothesis does not directly deal with a number of instances of aggressiveness. For one, some people express aggression when frustrated more readily than others do: Is this merely the result of past frustrations (including punishments), or have rewards for being aggressive played a part? For another, some people are aggressive with no apparent instigation: Is this a different form of aggressive behavior (sadism, say, as opposed to retaliation)? Are there still other forms of aggressiveness that people learn to use—socially acceptable aggression as against antisocial aggression, playful aggression versus serious attack, and so on?

Aggression has many outlets. It is often displaced, as when the family dog receives from a child the blow he has learned not to give his parents; it is attenuated, as when we retaliate to a blow by a sarcastic phrase or merely by entertaining an aggressive wish; it is projected, as when an aggressively aroused man refuses to admit his own aggression but sees others as aggressive, or when he calls others aggressive in order to justify a "peaceloving" aggressive act he has committed. A great deal of work needs to be done in specifying the subtle characteristics of effective *instigations* to aggression: Is aggression-in-anger less effective in eliciting counteraggression than aggression-in-cold-reason? Is injustice as vital as a physical blow in arousing aggression? Does the intention of the other person play an important part in arousing aggression; if so, what are the social conditions under which "malevolent intention" is inferred? What is the influence of mutual trust or distrust on the interpretation of an aggressive act? As for the *reduction* of aggression, there are many questions. Suppose B hits A but A is not permitted to hit back: Does this increase A's aggressive tendency? Suppose A does hit back: Does this decrease his aggressiveness or merely make him feel guilty? Suppose B hits A but C (for another reason) hits B: Does the sight or knowledge of this event reduce A's urge to be aggressive? These are only some of the many ramifications of the problem of aggression that have received attention in recent years. Let us turn to some of the studies that such questions have stimulated.

One of the principal questions psychologists have been asking about the socialization of aggression is this: How does a growing child pick up and in-

---

* L. Doob, *et al. Frustration and aggression.* New Haven: Yale University Press, 1939.

corporate in his repertoire of aggressions the aggressive properties and behavior of those around him? Some fascinating leads in this matter have been uncovered by Robert Sears * and his colleagues. Sears discovered that the most aggressive children are likely to come from homes where rules about aggressiveness are permissive but where punishment for acting aggressively is heavy. Conversely, the least aggressive children have been confronted with strong rules against aggression (which work to prevent it) but with nonpunitive means of dealing with it. Permissive rules apparently contribute more to making a child aggressive than heavy punishment does. Sears' information was limited to children at the ages of five and six as reported by the mothers themselves and must be applied only tentatively as yet to wider ranges of data.

Sears then followed a large number of these same children into adolescence † and again measured their aggressiveness by giving them a questionnaire. The questionnaire took into consideration many forms of aggressiveness possible by the age of 12: antisocial aggression, attenuated aggression, self-aggression, and projected aggression. The antisocial variety resembles the six year olds' aggression. Where parents maintain the same pressures on the children, high permissiveness still results in high aggressiveness at age 12; however, the heavily punished children now tend to be among the least antisocially aggressive.

This apparent shift between age 6 and age 12 in the effect of punishment may be considered in relation to one of the significant general theoretical insights of recent years. This is the notion: The dilemma posed by having aggressive tendencies while simultaneously fearing the consequences of acting on them produces a state called *conflict drive*. Where the conflict is great, because of a long history of being punished, a strong, or explosive, tendency toward aggressiveness will be evident at age six. But since by age twelve children who have been heavily punished tend to be among the least aggressive ones, continued punishment has presumably reduced conflict by leading the children, in effect, to give up antisocial aggression because of the very heavy inhibition now linked with it.

This principle of the drive, or tension, produced by conflict has been independently used in many contexts. Fritz Heider ** found it operating in the realm of ideas; Leon Festinger †† used it, as we will see later, in his brilliant analysis of the effects of "dissonance" following a decision; and Charles Osgood § used it in the study of "incongruity" created by different pressures for attitude change. Other versions and implications of the same notion are found in the works of other psychologists. In short, the idea of conflict drive

* R. R. Sears, E. E. Maccoby, and H. Levin. *Patterns of child rearing*. Evanston, Ill.: Row, Peterson, 1957.

† R. R. Sears. *J. abnorm. soc. Psychol.*, 1961, 63, 466–495.

** F. Heider. *The psychology of interpersonal relations*. New York: Wiley, 1958.

†† L. Festinger. *A theory of cognitive dissonance*. Evanston, Ill.: Row, Peterson, 1957.

§ C. Osgood, *et al. The measurement of meaning*. Urbana: University of Illinois, 1957.

in its various contexts and formulations is of general relevance to all phases of the study of socialization. Indeed, one basic theoretical problem now facing social psychologists is to determine which is the more powerful influence in human behavior: the reduction of conflict drive or the effects of direct rewards and punishments.

Attenuated aggression is a different matter from antisocial aggression: Among the 12-year-olds it tends to occur in a different group. It is common in highly punished children who have also lived under permissive aggression rules. Such "acceptable" forms of aggression emerge by age twelve when aggressive behavior has been inhibited earlier through successful punishments and so can be let out only in diluted form (and it comes out along with anxiety over being aggressive and some tendency toward self-aggression).

Sears also reports sex differences in aggressive tendencies: Boys resort more to the antisocial and girls to the attenuated variety. Girls, in fact, are generally less overtly aggressive. Girls also have more anxiety over being aggressive than boys do, and the two sexes here have divergent histories. This may be tied to genetic differences or to differences in other aspects of the handling of children of different sexes.

By now it should be clear that "aggression" is not a single, simple phenomenon. But we do have from Sears' work psychological leads to some of its components. We also have some hunches about how certain of these components show up in the behavior of the growing child.

Of course, the work of Sears is limited: limited in the number of children studied, in the measures used, in the weakness of the relationships discovered, and in geographical range. But it provides suggestive facts and examples of current theoretical notions. There are, as usual, alternative interpretations of the facts. It may be, for instance, that aggressive children are merely aping their punitive parents at age six, and that by twelve they drop antisocial for socially acceptable aggression because by then they have learned that the punishments by their parents are socially acceptable whereas their own past forms of aggression have not been. Or they may act aggressively in a permissive household on the rational supposition that they can get away with it. Or again, the findings may reflect changes in the public settings or changes in parental pressures as the child grows older. It may also reflect the effects of that mysterious business of identification that we mentioned in connection with the socialization of compliance. Let us turn briefly to the matter of useful ways of analyzing development of behaving like others. We will begin by considering the process of imitation.

Imitation

Some psychologists once thought of imitation as the simple, sovereign, and universal social psychological process that could explain most social behavior of men and animals. Imitation, it was often said, is part of human nature, an instinctual tendency to do what others do. But such a simple assumption hides complexity, as simple doctrines often do. Some people imitate more than others do, children imitate more than adults do, and people often do the opposite of what others do. Neal Miller and John Dollard * analyzed the problem of imitation in the context of social learning, demonstrating experimentally that it is possible for white rats (as well as children) to learn a habit of imitating if they are adequately rewarded for performing actions like the actions of other rats (or other children). Rewards increased the number of their early random acts of following so that they developed a tendency to follow the leader, and this tendency then generalized, or carried over, to some other situations and to some other leaders, as most habits do. Of course, with children, the leader might tell a follower the secret of knowing what to do, what the decisive cues were that led him to be correct. This is teaching, or copying, and though it may lead the second person to behave the same way as the first, it is not simple imitation. The same behavior might also occur because the two have learned in the past to respond similarly to the same cues, but this again is not necessarily due to simple and instinctual imitation. The relevant case, then, is called "matched-dependent behavior," the situation where a more learned leader's behavior is the cue to a less learned follower. The question here is: What are the conditions, if any, under which the follower will stop waiting for the actions of the leader and perform on his own?

Russell Church,† working with rats, has provided at least one answer to this question. Even these little creatures can pick up "incidental" cues that lead to the correct behavior, although they are not necessarily those the leader uses. That is, they occur naturally in such a way that they are present when a correct response is made but absent (or different) for an incorrect response. Let us use an example of a child's behavior with his mother to explain this notion. Suppose the child is following his mother walking on the stones in a creek bed; the mother avoids stones that are likely to be slippery because they have been covered by water. The child, however, learns to use gray stones but to avoid green ones (which happen also to be wet). Thus, when put into a similar situation all alone, he may behave correctly, even when his model is not there, by using the cue "greenness" in place of his mother's cue of "slipperiness." The child may have learned to do so whether he can say *what* he has learned or not; he has picked up the cues because they have been followed by success. In such a subtle way culture may sometimes be transmitted from older to younger—manners, skills, games, language habits and styles, and so on. And such differences in cues may be behind arguments that arise between generations.

Vicarious Socialization

Children *learn* habits of imitation, then, some more than others. Perhaps first-born children, who have extensive contact with expert, patient, and verbally active adults, learn this tendency more strongly than do later-born children, who deal more with

* N. E. Miller and J. Dollard. *Social learning and imitation.* New Haven: Yale University Press, 1941.
† R. Church. *J. compar. physiol. Psychol.,* 1957, 50, 3.

imperfect and impatient older children as models. Children also probably learn a habit of applying incidental cues (such as our example of "greenness"), learned from situations in which they have had models to follow, to other situations where models are not available. They do so, of course, with varying degrees of success in the new situations.

These habits are way-stations to the still richer possibilities of vicarious learning through observation. A simplified example of this occurs in a family or school when one child watches another child being taught and learns along with him. Seymour Berger * has experimentally demonstrated that under certain conditions the watcher's learning may equal or even exceed that of the person who is the actual and intended pupil, even though the watcher's successes and failures in learning got no observable feed-back. This may be because the imitative habits of the watcher are involved and he responds *covertly,* or internally (along with the person being taught, who is responding *overtly*), and is affected by his own covert successes and failures. Later, when the model is no longer there, the watcher is able to act overtly in line with these covertly learned responses.

Of course, we still have a great deal to learn about the conditions under which a watcher will vicariously practice the role of another, though it is probable that particularly favorable circumstances occur when the other is doing something the watcher values, when the other is a friend rather than enemy, and when both the cues and the other's responses are clear. When such possibilities have been studied we shall have forced into the open two important social psychological processes, imitation and vicarious learning.

Identification

Closely related to these two processes is *identification.* Often, in fact, these three strands are still not clearly differentiated, and there is as yet no standard terminology for the problems involved. The notion of identification has grown in part out of the rich soil of Freudian theory; some researchers even feel that the term should be applied only in psychiatric clinics to bizarre and apparently unconscious phenomena wherein a patient may have guilt over his feelings with regard to his parents.

Apparently, however, there exists a separable process we shall call identification. We see this process in action when a child behaves as if he had developed a desire or motive to feel like, act like, and think like a particular other person. Along with Church's notion of picking up incidental cues, this idea of identification casts light on occasions when a child learns, for example, to be like a parent without any apparent direct reward for so doing. This learning may be a simple matter of deciding covertly to practice the behavior of an important other person—but the intensity and results of this process are so great that to many researchers it is the most crucial issue in all of

* S. Berger. *Psychol. Rev.,* 1962, Vol. 69, No. 5, 450–466.

social psychology. We shall look at the results of some studies of this kind of behavior.

John W. M. Whiting * has recently brought forward a fruitful suggestion in his "envy" theory of identification. It is Whiting's notion that anyone, but particularly an unsophisticated child, wants to be like persons who induce a state of envy in him; it is his envy that leads the child covertly to practice the roles of these others. In a person's fantasies and daydreams he includes persons (parents or others) who normally give him things he wants and values, but these individuals are not the focus of the envy—they appear in the fantasies in their usual roles of providers, and not as persons the child would *like to be* or to replace. For instance, it is that parent who has proven his power to withhold resources the child has learned to value (food, money, affection, freedom from fear or pain, and so on) who will become the object of vicarious practice and therefore of covert learning. The indulgent parent is often surprised when his child begins to act like the restrictive parent, or temporarily, an unpleasant or fearful television character. Another example is provided by the business leader who maintains loyalty and efficiency in his subordinates by keeping a personal distance from them, thus increasing the value of his personal attention.

Of course, there is a great gap between covertly practicing the role of the person identified with and overtly playing it. Many a boy in American society has spent years alone with his mother while the father was away on business trips or in the army, and, even when the father is around, the mother may still maintain power over resources, power which is to be envied. Such a boy may covertly practice the mother's role but be shamed or punished by his friends or his mother herself if he behaves overtly in too feminine a manner. Thus, although such observational learning may remain as part of the growing boy's self-picture, it may never emerge as overt role-paying. It may show up only in rather subtle ways. For example, at Harvard's Laboratory of Human Development researchers started with the knowledge that on aptitude tests college men usually make higher quantitative scores than verbal scores, whereas college girls do the reverse. When the score patterns for college freshmen whose fathers had been away during World War II were compared to the scores of those whose fathers had always been at home it was found that the former had far smaller differences than the latter between verbal and quantitative scores—that is, they had a less masculine pattern. A replication of the study revealed that the degree of difference between the scores was directly related to the length of the father's absence—the smaller the difference, the longer the absence. These boys may well have taken on the *overt* masculine roles, though they still showed the influence of the covert female roles picked up when their mothers were the most powerful people around.

These findings highlight the powerful influence of imitation, vicarious

* J. W. M. Whiting. Resource mediation and learning by identification. In I. Iscoe and M. Stevenson (eds.). *Personality development in children.* Austin: University of Texas Press, 1960.

learning, and identification. Although these processes occur throughout life, they are probably particularly strong forces in the early years of socialization when one or two people appear to a child to have potent control over the things he needs and values. Never again, except in extreme circumstances, does so much depend upon so few; if such a situation *should* arise again, then conditions might be appropriate for basic personality changes.

In another study concerning identification, Lionel M. Lazowick * studied quantitatively the similarity between parents and their college-age children in emotional meanings of concepts. He held that this similarity is a measure of the strength of the subtle, sometimes still covert, identifications that exist among members of a family. He found that similarities in these emotional meanings were greater between fathers and sons than between fathers and daughters, but that similarities between mothers and daughters were no greater than between mothers and sons. Further, Lazowick related these similarities to a measure of the apparent general anxiety of the sons and daughters. It turned out that the less anxious boys have more meanings similar to those of both their mothers and fathers than do highly anxious boys. The trend is similar but not statistically reliable for girls. This finding reflects the importance of mothers in the socialization of American boys; it also suggests that cross-sex identification is not necessarily harmful, at least to the extent of arousing anxiety, to the boys concerned.

Conscience

Educators, parents, and people in general are all concerned with the development of *conscience*. But what do we really know about it? Winfred Hill † has made quite clear that a great deal of the "good behavior" from which we infer the strength of a person's conscience is really not very mysterious. Such behavior could well be learned simply through experiences with reward and punishment, through conditioning or learning to avoid some acts, or through various forms of vicarious learning. This is particularly true for learning to resist temptation even when parents or teachers are absent, and for developing habits of obeying the rules for good behavior.

The mysterious thing about conscience is why people behave in a guilty fashion when they have done what they ought not to have done. Hill points out that this behavior often involves self-criticism, a search for authorities who will accept a confession and apply punishments that supply relief, or a seeking out of some other form of punishment. We behave as if we wish to hurt ourselves—or arrange to get ourselves hurt by others—in payment for having "hurt a rule." This way, apparently, we can reduce the tensions arising from feelings aroused by the difference between what we have done and what we ought to have done. It has even been suggested that confession may

* L. M. Lazowick. *J. abnorm. soc. Psychol.,* 1955, 51, 175–183.
† W. F. Hill. *Psychol. Rev.,* 1960, 67, 317–331.

be so satisfying to some people that it serves to reinforce their habits of sinning.

An instructive empirical study by Robert Sears and his colleagues revealed an apparent relationship between strong conscience in a child and a history of having been disciplined with love-oriented techniques (such as praise, isolation, and the withdrawal of love) instead of either material-oriented methods (material rewards or the withdrawal of privileges) or physical punishment. Hill, though, finds this notion of "love-orientation" vague, as it certainly is, and has made the stimulating suggestion that the development of conscience may not have anything particular to do with "love" at all, but depends on the kind of learning that is rewarded when the "love-oriented" discipline is imposed. He suggests that a child who has done something wrong is put under parental disapproval until he has performed some *symbolic renunciation* of his wrongdoing, such as making an apology, making restitution, promising not to do the misdeed again, or taking personal blame. Then and only then is he let off the hook; the tension is thereby released and this release serves as a reward for the renunciation. When physical punishment is imposed or when privileges or material objects are withheld, no such requirement of renunciation is made of the child and the issue is resolved more quickly. This procedure is sometimes more comfortable for the child in the short run (and possibly in the long run as well), but it does less to strengthen his habits of renouncing and confessing.

Hill's suggestion deserves careful research study. It implies that parents may produce a strong "conscience" in a child with any form of discipline so long as symbolic renunciation is reinforced and maintained as an effective habit that eventually occurs *before* a wrong act is committed. This is no simple thing to achieve, but then neither is conscience, and we often either overshoot in creating too much of it, as Freud suggested, or in creating too little, as O. Hobart Mowrer reports he has often found in many mentally ill people. Despite these difficulties in practice, we are now on the threshold of important new advances in this age-old problem of the nature of conscience.

Stage Fright

Social psychologists take heed particularly of those strands of the socialization process that are most relevant to later social behavior. Certainly conscience, identification, and imitation have lasting consequences; less obviously, so does the process whereby a person develops sensitivity to audiences, whether he seeks to avoid them or exhibitionistically searches them out with delight.

Allan Paivio * has started to look carefully into the antecedents of audience sensitivity. Paivio measured stage fright in children by way of a specially designed questionnaire and then related this measure to information about the children's rearing obtained from their parents. When parents rewarded their

* A. Paivio, *et al. J. Personality*, 1959, 27, 1–17.

children frequently, punished them infrequently, and viewed their general social behavior favorably, the youngsters developed little stage fright. More pronounced degrees of stage fright were associated both with unfavorable parental evaluations of the children's social behavior and achievements and with frequent punishments for failure to meet parental standards. Imitation and identification also appear to be germane to the development of stage fright, since the children of sociable parents tend to be relatively unafraid of audiences. Exhibitionistic searching for audiences, which is apparently not the same thing as merely being unafraid, is not so clear to us in its development yet; but we do know that it is related to how positively parents evaluate a child's social comportment.

The usefulness of these two aspects of stage fright in predicting the actual behavior of children in front of audiences has been demonstrated by Alfred Baldwin and others.* They found that exhibitionism and self-consciousness both predict how long a child will talk before an audience. Children who are low on exhibitionism or high on self-consciousness (or both) tend to shorten their speaking times in public situations more than children at the opposite ends of the scales. On the other hand, children who are high on both, and who should therefore find the audience both a strong attraction and a thing of fear, make the most speech errors. These same measures predict the willingness of a child to participate in a public performance on skit night at camp.

These researches on "stage fright" and exhibitionism are a good example of two problems that fascinate social psychologists: how traits (stage fright, exhibitionism) develop in people as a result of social interaction, and also how these and other traits tend to function together in producing later more complicated behavior.

Affiliation

Recently, Stanley Schachter † boldly and profitably reopened an issue in the study of socialization that earlier researchers had found rather fruitless—that of birth order. He discovered (to his own surprise) in a study of some college students that a person's position in the birth order of his family is related to his choice of remaining alone or being with others when faced with a frightening situation. The preponderance of. persons who were first-born or only children reported that in a frightening situation they chose to be with others, whereas the preponderance of those who were later-born chose to face their worry alone. Of course, the degree of fright may be of importance in this relationship, and first-born and only children tend to have, or at least to report, greater fear. But even when only highly anxious people are considered, the same results related to order of birth are found. This effect Schachter found

---

* H. Levin, et al. J. abnorm. soc. Psychol., 1960, 61, 469–473.
† S. Schachter. The psychology of affiliation. Stanford: Stanford University Press, 1959.

shows up most clearly in an anxiety-producing or threatening situation. It is not related to family size, but it appears to be related to absolute order of birth in that a fourth-born person is even more likely to want to be alone than is a second-born one. These are clear and germinal findings, yet they were determined only after many other researchers had concluded that birth order was probably not a particularly significant source of differences in socialization.

Schachter was a good social psychological detective here, looking backward and forward, as well as carefully analyzing his findings. He looked back into the early period of personality formation to discover what there is about being first-born that might explain these differences. His best hunch, after reviewing past literature, is that dependency is highly developed in the first child by oversolicitous and inexperienced parents. He is given more care than later children and is more often breast-fed. Ratings of both boys and girls in a nursery school showed that first-borns tend to seek help, proximity, physical contact, attention, and recognition from adults more than do later-born children. Having developed these habits, the children may retain them and draw on them whenever they are anxious. This is a tentative interpretation, and there is need for further research here.

Schachter looked ahead to later behavior in which a difference in dependency might show up. He found indications that first-borns are more prone to utilize psychotherapy than are later-borns, the latter preferring to solve problems on their own. And other differences were detected. More later-borns are found among alcoholics than would be expected solely from their number in the population. Fewer fighter pilots who are first-born children become aces (with five or more kills), perhaps because of their higher anxiety. Harold H. Kelley * has recently pushed matters still farther with evidence suggesting that first-borns may handle power struggles in a manner different from that of later-borns. The former try to get their own way through means that will not alienate others, whereas the latter are more prepared to throw down the gauntlet and demand their own way, hang the consequences. The first-born seem to like to leave their adversaries feeling subordinated. This difference may stem from power strategies learned in the home: The first-born, as we have seen, is dependent and anxious and learns first to deal with unbeatable adults; the later-born, less dependent and less scared, learns early to deal with a first-born who can be frightened by a straight power-play. Schachter's findings, like all good science, casts light on old questions and gives us the opportunity to raise new ones.

Schachter has two suggestions regarding the value to first-borns in facing trouble with others rather than alone. First, the presence of others directly reduces his anxiety; second, he can satisfy his desire for self-evaluation by watching others and comparing his own response in the situation to theirs. "Know thyself" may be an admonition created by a first-born child.

* H. H. Kelley, *Report to NSF,* Grant NSF-G553, 1961.

Achievement Needs

One of the most far-ranging topics of social psychology today is the formation and function of the human need for achievement (if indeed it is a single need). David McClelland and John W. Atkinson * have led the research hunt on this issue, and just about every research technique available to social psychology has been thrown into the search, from measures of fantasy to controlled experiments, from phenomenological hunches to mathematical models, and sometimes all of these together.

David McClelland believes that achievement need can be measured by using the technique of the Thematic Apperception Test. Thus he provides a subject with some of the Thematic Apperception Test pictures and records the stories he makes up about the pictures. These stories are then analyzed by counting the number of times "themes" arise that pertain to "trying to do well with regard to standards of excellence." Although this measure is not ideally precise from a technical point of view, it has sparked a great deal of research and has even spawned a series of alternative methods of measurement. McClelland argues that his measures display the degree to which a person attempts to do well for the sake of a feeling of accomplishment, and that those who strive for success because they want to do well can be distinguished from those who are merely out for money or recognition.

Some of the research on this need for achievement has focused on its development. The origin appears to be early in a child's life—it is fairly well developed by the age of eight or ten. Marian R. Winterbottom † has pointed out that it occurs more frequently and strongly in families that give children opportunity, or even pressure, to be independent and self-reliant early. Such children are expected to tie their shoes early in life; they are prepared to try to fix their own bikes if they break down.

Bernard Rosen and Roy D'Andrade ** went into the homes of both boys of this sort and boys low in achievement need. They discovered that both the mothers and the fathers of the former set higher goals for their sons in experimental tasks and reacted more positively to their sons' performance than did the parents of the others. Most interestingly, however, mothers of the high-need boys were more domineering than the mothers of the low-need boys, but the trend among the fathers was the other way around. In short, fathers who help produce a strong achievement motive in boys set high goals and are warm and positive about their sons' performances but they step aside and let the boys try things on their own and follow their own initiative.

In our discussion of culture and personality in Chapter 7 we shall say something about the implications for a society of having a large number of people with high achievement needs. It is an exciting area of social

* D. C. McClelland. *The achieving society*. Princeton: D. Van Nostrand Co., 1961.

† I. L. Child. Socialization. In G. Lindzey (ed.). *Handbook of social psychology*. Reading, Massachusetts: Addison-Wesley Co., 1954, Vol. 3, pp. 655–692.

** B. C. Rosen and R. D'Andrade. *Sociometry,* 1959, Vol. 22, No. 3, 185–218.

psychology, one that points to another, and very important, kind of social process—economic development—which in part has its roots in socialization.

We have discussed some of the factors that appear to be involved in the socialization of people and we have looked at some of the products of socialization. We need to remind ourselves that socialization does not end with childhood but is continuously shaping and moulding people throughout their lives. Some of the effects of early pressures and experiences last all our lives; others are short-lived and become overlaid by new learnings or new requirements that the public and private settings of our lives place upon us. But we probably change less easily as time passes and experiences pile up: Each person develops stronger traits and more subtle defenses *vis à vis* the world just at the time that it becomes harder for other persons to exert the control needed to give rise to imitation, identification, and vicarious reinforcement.

Socialization, then, is a huge process that we understand only in part, having as we do information only about "this and that" rather than about the "whole thing." But the evidence we do have suggests that the general process of socialization will some day rank with genetic endowment and personal development as one of the great makers of man, creating both differences and similarities.

We must recognize, however, that a great deal of our knowledge about the socialization of personality comes from America and from other countries of Western civilization. This is both understandable and useful to us, but our intellectual ethnocentrism is beginning to crumble under the impact of the growth of social psychology in other world areas. Furthermore, American social psychologists are starting to study other places when they travel.

We outlined some pancultural dimensions of differences in the handling of children earlier in this chapter. These factors emerged after a study of socialization practices in six widely different areas of the world. This costly research procedure was undertaken because of an awareness of the great differences in those practices that shape people to conform to the values of those around them.

We shall therefore return, in our last chapter, to the question of what the socialization process is in our search for understanding the broad issue of how personality is related to culture and society. It is on a world scale that we shall see the shape of the general socialization process most clearly, and it is exactly a world perspective that is emerging in social psychology.

Before tackling such large problems, however, we must look still more closely at the fine texture of social behavior. To begin, in the next chapter we shall focus on the ubiquitous process of perceiving and judging the social world, keeping in mind as we must that each person's socialization contributes to, but is also greatly affected by, the particular form and content of the momentary social situations, tasks, and roles in which he finds himself.

Perceiving and Judging
Social Events

So far we have been concentrating on rather large-scale, diffuse social influences—identification, aggressiveness, compliance, conscience, and so on. Now we want to turn our gaze to the other end of the scale, to see in finer texture how human beings cope with their social world. Our main theme in this chapter will be how we use the immediate information available in social situations in perceiving and interpreting those situations. Although socialization does determine in part how people use such information, so that we cannot therefore entirely escape considering personality determinants, still our purpose is to examine the short-

28

3

term mechanisms of social perception. Our main aim is to describe what we know about how social information is *received* (that is, how social stimuli are interpreted) as well as how such information is *sent* (either intentionally or unintentionally).

Let us pause here just a moment to face up to one difficulty from the outset. The same physical-social information can often be interperted in a number of ways. The noises of a cocktail party betoken joy to one person, fear to another. A pleasant grin on the face of a friend is satisfying to one person, but a disappointment to someone who hoped to see a much broader smile of welcome. Such are the empirical problems of social perception encountered in trying to discover in just how many ways the same stimulus situation can be "received." In research on such matters, it is important, also, to maintain sufficient control over (or systematic variation of) the motivations and habits of subjects to be able to evaluate the causal power of the immediately present information on their percepts and judgments. It may be the case, for example, that the murmur of human voices that accompanies a party may *always* be pleasant to any new arriver. But this common pleasantness may be lost because it disappears into the welter of other unknown or uncontrolled feelings and wishes the new arrivals bring with them.

Further, there may be many ways to send information in order to achieve the same perception or judgment. You can make a man see that he is not wanted in a number of different ways. There are also probably several ways to prove to others that you are a bright, ambitious, all-American boy. This variability, too, raises problems for research in social psychology. In the pages that follow, therefore, we will often be reporting on only *some* of the informational conditions that effect "most people" in a particular way, or on *some* of the conditions under which a particular kind of information is sent. We are not yet able to be exhaustive in this field—we simply lack the knowledge to do so.

It is worth noting, also, that the conditions for accurately receiving information are often very different from those for sending the same kind of information. It is one thing to spot the movements and intonations which mean that someone is about to criticize you, but these are not the same movements or intonations which would move the actor to decide that the criticism was called for. In the examples which follow we will keep separate the conditions of *perceiving* X from the conditions for *sending* X, though both are of interest to social psychologists.

ON FAILURE OF PERCEPTION

Social psychologists Eunice Cooper and Marie Jahoda * have prepared some cartoons featuring a "Mr. Biggot" which lampoon bigotry in such a

* E. Cooper and M. Jahoda. *J. Psychol.*, 1947, 23, 15–25.

way that most readers find them funny. It is doubly (and rather frighteningly) humorous, however, when an observer who is extremely bigoted sees them as upholding bigotry rather than satirizing it! Many times indeed a person's failure to perceive social events accurately strikes us as funny. Often, too, such failures are sad, even tragic, as when a well-intentioned sheriff does not note accurately enough when an angry group turns into a lynch mob.

A practical joker enjoys placing others into unperceived or unexpected situations. Similarly, a manipulator of a mob, leader of the political power play, a person who aims to break a horse—all have the same general intent: to engineer a change so that it is not perceived in time, or at all, by the person "under control." The mob is aroused by quietly passed vicious rumors so that the sheriff will not see the growing anger. The power of the opposition is cut away by secret negotiation until the hour of the final vote so that the actual state of affairs will not be recognized. The horse is lured to compliance by the successive addition of ever heavier things to his back (cloth, then blankets, then a saddle, finally a man) before his vigilance against change can be aroused.

Social psychologists aim to discover more about the everyday conditions that lead to both accurate and inaccurate judgment of such social events as those mentioned above as well as such events as states of emotion in others, the intentions of those around us, and the presence of hierarchical social orders in the groups of which we are members.

THE PROBLEM OF PERCEPTION

Our perceptions are sometimes treated as very special and mysteriously private occurrences that have to do with what we "really see, hear, or feel" as different from what we *do about* the things we see, hear, or feel. In fact, we should perhaps talk of perception only when the event or object being perceived is actually present to the perceiver, and we should talk of another process—cognition, for example—when the observer is judging or recalling some object or event of the recent past. We shall use the term more loosely to refer to both of these kinds of occurrence.

There is also some doubt that perceptions of social events are in fact a special class of occurrences. Donald Campbell * of Northwestern University has recently suggested that there is often a very close tie between how we tend to see something and what we tend to do about it. In fact, "how I see" something may merely be an alternative way of reporting what "I am about to do" about the same thing. When we report that we see atomic war as "threatening" we are at the same time stating that we are prepared to act and vote in ways that will avoid war. When in football a coach sends in his best left end

* Donald Campbell, in S. Koch (ed.). *Psychology, a study of a science.* New York: McGraw-Hill, 1963, Vol. VI.

to counter the opponent's right end, he is at the same time displaying his perception of the "excellence" of the opponent. Perceiving is a way of acting that has close relations to other ways of acting.

For research purposes, therefore, we consider that a subject has perceived something when he consistently *talks or otherwise acts* differently in that "something's" presence (or recent presence) under conditions where the researcher has independently checked or varied the presence of the something. For example, a clever experimenter can alter the informal structure of a group by adding to it a very dominating person. He can check the perception of this change by either noting consistent (and reasonable) changes in the behavior of the other members of the group, or by asking these members to make verbal statements about the changed relations among them. Some insensitive members of the group may note no change and act no differently; others may immediately detect, behaving accordingly, that a new social event has occurred.

We should at once note that there is a great challenge in this kind of study: how to achieve control over the occurrence of a social event so that the conditions of its perception can be studied. Such control calls for much ingenuity and, increasingly, much use of new equipment and social illusion on the part of the researchers. Yet, there is a limit to what can be achieved by way of creating, even with the best equipment and the most bold use of illusion, even the *apparent* occurrence of social events. It is still more difficult to create the *actual* occurrence of some social events. We can only go so far in causing mobs to form, rebellions to arise in a small group. And we can hardly create even the illusion of a revolution. It becomes evident that our research in social perception has hardly begun, particularly when we see that we must systematically vary the occurrence of a social event in order to discover what information about it is necessary to enable the average person to perceive it.

There is also little doubt that great individual differences exist in the speed and accuracy of spotting a social event or a change in a situation because such judgments rest to so great a degree on past learning. Thus, it is difficult in a research setting to decide when a quick spotting of a social event results from the information being varied by the experimenter or from old habits of attention or interest of the subject. The rebellious son of a dominating father may see the dominating quality of a new group member at once; the trouble is that he may see *any* new member as dominating until proved otherwise.

Despite these problems, our interest here is to report some attempts to discover the information *anybody* needs to spot social events. Much research energy has been applied to the task of uncovering the way the past learning, needs, and biases of individuals affect their use of social information. Our discussion will touch on examples of such internal sources of judgments, but we are mainly interested in cases that may cast light on the necessary conditions for *accurate* social judgments.

The direction a person looks can be a social event, and as such it seems simple enough, yet it plays a critical role sometimes in interpersonal behavior. In games and sports the direction of a person's eyes may give away the direction of his next action. Children are extremely sensitive to being looked at; rhesus monkeys register a change in electrical potential from the brain-stem when people look at them.

Looking at someone is an observable action that can be engineered for experimental purposes in a direct and simple manner. James Gibson and Ann Danielson * trained a woman to place her eyes precisely in any one of seven positions relative to an observer, and to place her head in any one of *three* positions. One of the eye positions was fixation on the middle of the observer's forehead and one of the head positions was directly facing the observer. The "looker" kept her face impassive to rule out additional clues, and, it is reported, she had "very large brown eyes." Each observer was then asked to state (for all these conditions, randomly varied) whether he was being looked at directly.

Despite poor illumination, observers made very few errors; in fact, their acuity in judging the looker's line of regard was at least equal to that in discriminating fine print on a visual acuity chart in an oculist's office. Of course, more errors were made when the line of regard was "askance," as when her face was pointed to the left while her eyes fixed on the forehead of the observer.

It is useful to note here the difference between the conditions for *receiving* information about being looked at and those for *sending* the information "I am looking at you." Many Americans who have "skoaled" in true Scandinavian fashion feel some embarrassment when they are first called upon to hold the line of regard mutually with a person of the opposite sex while each downs a drink. They must learn to control an act (looking at another) that is usually left to expressive spontaneity. Or is it?

Ralph Exline † has recently begun to study some of the conditions under which this "mutual visual interaction" occurs apparently "spontaneously." He first measured 48 subjects for their usual spontaneous tendency to gaze into another's eyes. Then he retested them after they had been embarrassed by being implicated in cheating while working jointly with another person, who was a confederate of the experimenter. While being interrogated about this event, subjects tended to look directly at the interrogator less often than they had before. One particularly suggestive discovery the researchers made was that subjects whose answers to a questionnaire showed them to be

---

* J. Gibson and A. Danielson. *Amer. J. Psychol.* (to be published Fall, 1963).

† Ralph Exline, *et al. Amer. Psychol.*, 1961, Vol. 16, No. 7, 396.

high on "Machiavellianism" in their attitudes toward other people, changed far less between tests than did those who were low on "Machiavellianism." A high score of Machiavellianism means that a person is more ready than most to manipulate other people for practical ends. Apparently the traits of a person must be taken in conjunction with the situation of the embarrassing interrogation in future predictions of whether he will spontaneously gaze directly into another person's eyes.

It would be instructive to investigate whether people who make the most errors in receiving information about another's line of regard are low Machiavellians who may have had less practice in staring at others. Our main point should be clear, however: In studying the conditions for receiving a certain kind of information (like being looked at) it is fruitful as well to study the conditions for sending that same information (looking at another, or looking mutually at one another), since both occur, sometimes simultaneously, in everyday life. And the conditions for one may be interwoven with the conditions for the other.

Another point should be clear: We have hardly begun to ask the intriguing questions involved in even this "simple" form of interplay. Gibson, after all, studied just "being looked at"; Exline studied "looking into the line of regard of another." But what are the physical and personality conditions under which we send or receive such acts as "peering," "glancing," "glowering," "contemplating," "looking bashfully or covertly," "letting the gaze wander," and so on? Obviously, a "bashful look" depends for its *reception* on more than the geometry of the line of regard since it depends on some facial expression, and it probably usually depends on some other trait than Machiavellianism for its *occurrence*.

THE PERCEPTION OF FACIAL EXPRESSION

People usually judge the line of regard in the context of facial expression, so it is sensible to look at what we know about how we perceive expressions. Photography has provided psychologists with a way to engineer information about faces by systematically varying facial features in pictures. Foam rubber and plastics promise an even more flexible way of physically engineering facial expressions, but work has just begun (largely at Cornell) on this approach to the study of what James Gibson calls the information carried by deformations of rubbery surfaces such as a face. For the most part now, we still rely on photographs.

Pictures are a far cry from the complex actuality of daily life, but they are a starting place, and through the use of them in recent years we have come to some understanding of what facial forms lead observers to agree about what emotion is being expressed. This does not mean that the emotion *observed* is the emotion felt or that the emotion felt is the one that is *displayed*—we know even less about the accuracy of emotional communication between persons. But delineating *that* social process has awaited the increase in knowledge about the simpler situation of judging facial expression. In the usual procedure an observer looks at a picture of a face and either tells what he sees there, or merely rates the photograph on a pre-arranged scale.

The most popular scale is that of Robert Woodworth, who reduced a good many of the English terms for describing emotional expression to certain common categories and constructed this scale: a) love, happiness, and mirth; b) surprise; c) fear and suffering; d) anger and determination; e) disgust; f) contempt; and g) a residual category. Woodworth showed that judges very rarely disagreed by more than one category in evaluating the same picture. Harold Schlosberg * elaborated on this work and developed a theory that really only three dimensions are needed for describing all facial expressions: degrees of pleasantness vs. unpleasantness, degrees of acceptance vs. rejection, and degrees of arousal. Harry Triandis and W. W. Lambert † found supportive evidence for this view in a rural Greek community, and Arthur Wolf and W. W. Lambert have evidence from Formosa that shows that even monolingual Taiwanese villagers judge and place the photographs of an American girl in pretty much the same way that college students at Brown University do. It may be that even though Formosans are trained to display (or "send") facial expressions less often or in a more muted manner than Americans, when they do they use their faces in somewhat similar ways.

Work has only begun on the social and personality conditions for *sending* facial expression information spontaneously or in a studied manner the way some actors do. Why do people with diverse cultural backgrounds agree that some facial patterns show "determination," or that Mickey Mouse (an international star) is "cute"? Is the basis for such common judgments learned through some common experience? Does it depend merely on a cultural stereotype (the universality of the cross-cultural evidence throws some doubt on this possibility)? Or do such judgments reflect primitive facial expressions that under certain spontaneous conditions, do in fact "express emotions"? If this last is true, then Schlosberg's dimensions may be the basic dimensions of our actual feeling states and thus provide us with a theory of emotions *per se* (as he thinks), as well as giving us a theory regarding the conditions for agreement in the perception of emotions.

FORMING IMPRESSIONS OF OTHERS

The characteristic ways a person uses his line of regard and his face to express emotions or self-consciously to send information are socially important in part because they permit another person to form impressions of his personality. Such impressions in turn, are practically important—as every

* H. Schlosberg. *Psychol. Rev.*, 1954, 61, 81–88.
† H. Triandis and W. W. Lambert. *J. abnorm. soc. Psychol.*, 1958, Vol. 56, No. 3, 321–382. Also, A. Wolf and W. W. Lambert, unpublished manuscript, 1963, Cornell University.

politician or statesman knows—since people use them to predict a sender's future behavior and to determine their own behavior in response.

Research on the formation, or "reception," of impressions is in its infancy but has already seen a number of developments. For one, Solomon Asch * investigated the role of language. He asked subjects to write down their imaginative impressions of a person described as "industrious—skillful—intelligent—warm—determined—practical—cautious." Another group heard the same description with the single change of "cold" in place of "warm." The impressions were markedly different between groups; apparently each group organized its pieces of information into a whole, and in doing so focussed on certain "central" traits (like warmth and coldness), but gave scant attention to "peripheral" traits (such as politeness and bluntness). The form of the final impression is a whole that not only is more than the sum of its parts but also cannot be derived or predicted from the separate bits of information provided. It is possible to vary "received impressions" by careful manipulation of the known "peripherality" or "centrality" of the trait words, but how the final impression emerges from the variations is still unknown in Asch's theory.

Julius Wishner † has recently helped to dispel much of the mystery that surrounds Asch's notion of impression formation. He, too, had groups read brief adjectival descriptions of people that were systematically varied; he then asked his subjects to record their impressions by making out a longer check list of adjectives to show what the described person would be like. He shows that the final impression *can* be predicted fairly well from a knowledge of the relations that exist between the trait names that are varied and the traits on the check list which are to be judged on the basis of the final impression. Wishner shows that a peripheral trait can be made central if the check list includes a number of items closely related to it. Suppose we give one group a list of adjectives that includes "blunt" and give another group the same list with "polite" substituted for "blunt." The resultant impression of the first group will show a central effect for "blunt"; they will organize their impression around that notion, tending to check items such as "unkind, critical, hard, unbending," but the effect will be peripheral on such items as "scrupulous, persuasive, strong, popular." With the second group of subjects, "polite" will organize the impression when the subject is given an opportunity to check such items as are in the second group of adjectives.

Each verbal item of information, then, adds up to make the impression, within the context of what the subject is set to make judgments about. Knowing the information received by the subject *and* what he is set or asked to judge about the other, we can predict the content of his judgment or impression. The wise "impression-sender" must try to control both these factors. It does little good for an advertiser to show how "fragrant and polite" his

* S. E. Asch. *J. abnorm. soc. Psychol.*, 1946, 41, 258–290.
† J. Wishner. *Psychol. Rev.*, 1960, Vol. 67, No. 2, 96–112.

soap product is if the listener is waiting to judge how rough and effective it is. The experimenter (and to some extent, the advertiser) can control the "set" of the subject, but it is more difficult to *predict* what set will occur under everyday conditions. The social psychology of interpersonal perception will be still more advanced when Wishner's findings are cross-related to research on subjects' wants and interests which will help to predict the subjects' set. This is a large order for future research.

Although Asch-like effects have been shown when actual people rather than verbal descriptions of people have been used in experimental conditions, the *total* range of information available for impression formation has not been systematically varied. Some explorations have been made, however, into the conditions of "empathizing" with the feelings and judgments of others. Urie Brofrenbrenner and colleagues * found that at least two skills, or empathic abilities, underlie success in this endeavor: sensitivity to the "generalized other," or the *average* feeling or judgment of a group of persons, and sensitivity to the feelings and judgments of *specific* individuals.

Empathy is a very complicated research area and is fraught with many fascinating pitfalls, for subjects may appear to be empathetic when they are actually judging on some other basis than the immediate information received. For example, it is often possible to guess what, say, five people think about some topic without ever having met these people at all, particularly if you know what general opinion on the topic is and you know this group is a "randomly selected group." You can even be correct better than chance on guessing about the individual *personalities* of, say, five students you have not even met. This better-than-chance performance cannot be due to any empathic ability aroused by specific information about these specific people. In short, it is difficult to rule out the effects of stereotypes that *happen* to be partly correct in order to focus on what information from others leads to accurate empathizing or impression formation.†

The other side of empathy has not been studied directly as yet, though its practical importance is recognized. This question is, how does a person communicate empathy? Some people have control over this ability: They leave others with the distinct impression that they understand and feel akin to them even when they are not in fact empathic. Some leave others cold in this regard. Skills or manners of sending information about empathy (or even the illusion of it) may underlie the success of a politician, a salesman, or a therapist. Some of this skill may rest in matching in one's aspect and action an individual's particular learned *conception* of an empathic person; some of it may result from subtle actions that in fact betoken empathy to *any* human being. In any case, we can by experiment eventually discover the kinds of information necessary or sufficient for the judgment that "this person

* U. Brofrenbrenner, J. Harding, and M. Gallwey. Chapter II in D. McClelland, *et al. Talent and society*. Princeton: D. Van Nostrand, 1958.
† L. J. Cronbach. *Psychol. Bull.*, 1955, 52, 177–193.

understands me." The equation for the "good bedside manner" lies over the next research hill.

Intentions

The communication of empathy presents a complicated problem, but for the simpler task of judging whether a person has benevolent or malevolent *intentions* some progress has recently been made. Alfred Baldwin and Nina Lambert * have devised a way of predicting whether another person will be judged malevolent or benevolent. They do so by taking into consideration some things about the judge, along with the information he receives about some crucial social choices made by the other.

Suppose, for example, that you are P and must judge the intention of O when he chooses between certain alternative actions. For instance, if O is given a choice between an action that would benefit both him and you (P^+O^+) and one that would benefit himself but harm you (P^-O^+) and he chooses the first, is he intending to help you or harm you? Suppose he chooses P^-O^+ over P^+O^+? Suppose he chooses P^-O^+ over P^+O^-?

It is possible to predict quite accurately the judgments by college students of the degree of benevolence or malevolence in 16 such abstract situations, but the prediction requires a rather complicated theory. Baldwin feels the theory is based on the "naive" beliefs about the psychology of others that we use in everyday life. In short, judges use a number of *assumptions* in determining whether O is kind or cruel, assumptions that are generally enough held by mature Americans to serve as a "cultural code" for thinking through such problems. Americans (and possibly people in other nations) assume, for example, that if the two alternatives open to O are identical, then O's selection (for instance, P^-O^- versus P^-O^-) gives no information about his intention. We also assume that others prefer to benefit themselves rather than harm themselves, other things equal, and that people prefer to choose the alternative that results in the *same* outcomes for both of those who are involved, rather than different outcomes, other things equal. There is evidence that these assumptions are learned at different ages: For example, the first assumption mentioned above has not been learned by four or five years of age, so a child of that age sees O as benevolent when he chooses P^+O^+ over P^+O^+, and malevolent when he chooses P^-O^- over P^-O^-.

This general approach may provide a nice way to discover the bases of differences in our perceptions of different social roles: Is a Senator judged

---

* A. Baldwin and N. Lambert. "Judgments of benevolence and malevolence." Ithaca: Cornell University, 1962 (mimeographed report).

more or less benevolent when he (as O) chooses P^-O^- over P^-O^+ than a father would be?

Baldwin stresses that *learned codes* assist us in making judgments of the intentions of other people, but direct information about O's choice is also instrumental. Indeed, most judgments of complex social events probably are interpretations of immediate information in terms of codes learned in other, perhaps earlier similar situations. Thus does the jury judge the criminal, the sheriff predict the mob. Delineating the codes (cultural or personal) and specifying the information that are necessary and sufficient for consistent (and sometimes even "correct") perceptions and judgments make a more complicated problem than social psychologists might wish, but it is not insoluble.

Social Causality

Related to Baldwin's work are the experiments of John Thibaut and Henry Riecken * on the judgment of causation. Consider yourself a subject in their experiment. You are a college freshman. You come to a laboratory where you meet two other persons who have also apparently come to participate in a social-psychological experiment. One of them turns out to be a neatly dressed Ph.D., an instructor, the other a rather sloppy freshman. Actually, they are confederates of the experimenter. You are asked by the experimenter to try to persuade these people to donate blood for a Red Cross drive. You do so by sending messages to the two other people, who have been put into another room, supposedly to "rule out personal face-to-face persuasion." Eventually each one complies with your requests, simultaneously and in the same way. The research question is: What, in your judgment brought about the compliance in each case? The finding: If you are like most subjects tested, you would decide that the high-status Ph.D. complied because he was a nice person; the freshman did so because he was convinced by the force of your argument. Further, because of your perceptions of why they have complied, you would tend to have a more positive attitude toward the high-status person who has complied because he's a "nice guy" than toward the low-status person who gave in because you forced him. In this situation, in short, the cause of compliance is perceived as "external" to the lower-status person, "internal" to the higher-status one.

Note how in this study one judgment is related to an earlier one; that is, *perceived causality* depends on the *perceived status* of the other person. Thibaut and Riecken had trouble, though, in manipulating the situation so that all subjects put the right person in the right status. The two confederates, for the purposes of the experimental control, shifted back and forth in the roles they played. One of them happened to be relaxed and soft-spoken, the other more formal and stern. Thus, when the latter took the high-status role, status discrimination was easy for the subject, but when the soft-spoken actor took that role, the distinction was not so clearly made since the "naturally"

* J. Thibaut and H. W. Riecken. *J. Person.*, 1955, 24, 113–133.

more "powerful" personality was trying to play the lowly freshman and the "naturally" more "easy-going" person was trying to be a lordly Ph.D.! An error in the perception of status tended to have effects on the perception of causality in a manner consistent with the main findings of the study.

The practical value of this study is displayed by a follow-up experiment by Lloyd Strickland.* Here subjects served as supervisors of the work of two subordinates, who again were really confederates of the experimenter in an experiment supposedly on work supervision. The work of both subordinates was equal in all cases, but the supervisor was permitted more surveillance over the work of subordinate A than he was over the work of subordinate B. This had two effects: First, the supervisor came to trust subordinate B's motivation to work more than he did subordinate A's. This was because he thought B "liked the work" for internal reasons ("he is a conscientious person"), whereas A worked *because* he was watched. Second, when given a chance later to watch over these subordinates equally, the subject supervisor *chose* on his own to continue the differential surveillance foisted on him at the beginning.

Thibaut and Riecken believe that the principle of social perception involved here has further consequences. Consider, they suggest, what happens when a tyrannical government attempts to get compliance from its citizens. First the tyrannous leaders may push the people around. Then, the more they see that they are "forcing" compliance through external pressure the less they can perceive spontaneous, loyal compliance based on affection (internal causality). This judgment leads to ever more forceful use of power, which in turn still further decreases the chance of perceiving spontaneous, secure compliance. And on the cycle may go until rebellion occurs. These may be very important social-psychological ideas indeed!

We must be aware, however, of the problems that lurk in all these experiments. For one, even when experiments are carefully designed and carefully performed, all human beings do not behave as the principle says that they should. Some people fail to see that a Ph.D. instructor has more power or status than a freshman; some who do manage to detect the status difference do not perceive the high-status person as giving in from internal causes. A few even see the high-status one as only giving in when pushed into it! Social psychologists are in constant search of ways of cutting down such sources of wobble in their studies, or of recognizing some of these sources as discoveries in their own right.

Many studies, for example, purport to show that a person views those who have influence over him as likeable. Renato Tagiuri and others † have, however, thoughtfully pointed out that as a matter of empirical fact, there are at least four patterns of such relationships: 1) some persons like best those with whom they share mutual influence; 2) others like best those they feel that

* L. Strickland. *J. Person.*, 1958, 26, 200–215.
† R. Tagiuri and N. Kagan. *J. Person.*, 1960, Vol. 28, No. 3.

they influence; 3) some like best those who influence them; and 4) some subjects display only a weak relationship between preference and influence. We must constantly beware of the easy over-generalization in matters as slippery as social perception.

Social Hierarchies

Although cultural and personal codes often help us to make some useful or true social discriminations, we do tend to use them inappropriately. At the risk of getting sidetracked into "misperception" rather than searching out the conditions for accurate perception, let us consider the problem of learning to perceive, judge, and remember *social structures*.

Plainly, real-life social structures come in all shapes and sizes and with diverse relationships holding them together. Consider for the moment only four-person groups (and let us limit ourselves to four *men* in order to keep down the usual complexities added by sex differences). In one such group, the *influence structure* may have this pattern: A influences B, C and D; B influences C and D; and C influences D. In short, a simple chain-of-command ordering of influence exists, like that in a formal military situation. Another group may be the same except that B has no influence over C and D. Or, again, it may be that A can influence B and *vice versa,* and that C can influence D and vice versa, but that there is no influence from one pair to the other. Finally (but by no means exhaustively) the scheme may be A→B→C→D, along with A→D, D→B, and C→A. The possible varieties of such structures in the social world are vast, and all of us have met many of them, whether we perceived them or not.

Clinton De Soto * has done experiments which suggest that college students have a tendency to be alert to power-based orderings like the first (military) example above. In his experiments he worked out all the possible relations among people involved in these various structures, gave names to Messrs. A, B, C and D, and put each relation on the back of a card (for example, "John influences Jim"). On the front of each card he placed a question such as: "Does John influence Jim or does he not?" The task for subjects was to learn the answers to all the questions for each structure in turn in as few trials as possible, by trying to answer each question, then turning the card over to see whether he was correct. De Soto's hunch was borne out—the first structure exemplified above was by far the easiest to learn, and it took almost three times as many trials (on the average) to learn the correct answer to the same number of cards which represented the *last* structure suggested above.

De Soto believes that it is a widespread human tendency in judging (or learning) influence structures to use a code (or schema, as he prefers to call it) that finds order even when it does not exist, and that leaves structures like the last one above in some sense "unnatural." He even goes so far

* C. B. De Soto. *J. abnorm. soc. Psychol.,* 1960, 60, 417–421.

as to suggest that such a code may come to act as a *social expectation*. We expect a group to have a simple pecking order and, if this expectation is shared by others in the group, a pecking order will emerge where one did not "need" to exist otherwise. Such a suggestion is certainly worthy of research by people, like Americans, who say that they prefer democratic structures to top-down ones.

We should also report that this tendency toward perceiving simple order does not hold for other aspects of social structures such as relations of confiding and liking. In fact, people tend to expect relations of confidence to be symmetrical: when A confides in B, B will be expected to confide in A.

Social Contribution

A recent study by Henry Riecken * points up both the difficulties involved in doing clear research on the judgment of social events and the beginning we are making in solving these difficulties. Riecken investigated the matter of how credit is assigned for contributing good ideas in a group discussion. Common experience and a number of early studies would suggest that the talkative member of a group often gets a good deal of credit from the others, more than he deserves.

Now, the earlier studies on this problem kept a reliable, objective record of only one element—talkativeness (which is easy to count). The actual quality of suggestions made by the talkative people (and others) was left to vary naturally and was "measured" by the judgments of the group members themselves, not perhaps the most accurate judges.

Riecken devised a means of varying experimentally both the quality of contribution and the contributor. In his experiment, four-man teams discussed problems in human relations. One such problem had a unique and elegant solution, one that was hard to discover without help. The experimenter, during the discussion, passed a hint on to either the most talkative member of the group or to the least talkative. The chosen person could then bring it up for discussion and possible acceptance.

When he gave the hint to the talkative member, the others always accepted it as the best solution, except when the talkative person was not really convinced that the solution was a good one. When the hint-holder was a quiet sort, the others rarely accepted the hint unless it got the backing of someone more talkative (usually the *second most* talkative member, who often acts in many groups as a specialist in handling personal feelings).

Later, group members were asked to judge "who contributed most to the solution of the problem." When the top talker had held the hint, and managed to get it accepted, he got credit for it 82 per cent of the time. When the low talker got it accepted, he received recognition only 60 per cent of the time. Further, the top talker was almost uniformly seen as having contributed more than the low talker, and other data show that he does indeed tend to be more

* H. W. Riecken. *Sociometry*, 1958, 21, 309–321.

effective in getting people to go along, though he is not any better at coping with opposition to his suggestions.

It appears, then, that group members are fairly accurate in judging contributions to a discussion, though there is some bias in giving credit to the heaviest contributor as the best contributor. This judgment is often true, however, in that someone who makes frequent suggestions does manage to get a high-quality idea accepted more often. There may well be good sense in the judgmental bias in terms of long-run pay-off probabilities: The judgment "the high talker gives the best ideas" is most often correct. Most people appear to work under some such assumption. Here again is a case of judgment based on both immediate information and a set of habits in judging.

The Riecken study stretched our experimental grasp with the discovery of how to manipulate the quality of contribution. Steps are now under way at a number of research centers to manipulate the talkativeness of the subjects as well. One way this can be done is by secretly letting a subject know that the experimenter (or, presumably though not actually, the rest of the group) thinks he is speaking very well and to the point. In this way an untalkative person can be rendered talkative, and, more humanely, perhaps, the talkative ones can be shut up. Once this technique is worked out satisfactorily, experimenters can return to Riecken's problem and systematically vary both conditions for the perception of contributions—quality and quantity.

Judgments of Majorities

Consider the problem of a group chairman or politician in trying to estimate which side has a majority on a controversial issue. Research by Leon Levy * suggests that college students (and possibly other people as well) judge the existence of a majority in rather consistent ways. In a group that split 20–20 on some issue, the students tended to say that a split of 30–10 would be needed to betoken a clear majority. The ratio between the size of the needed change and the size of the evenly split group tended to remain constant (particularly with larger groups); thus, a 200–200 division would have to become a 300–100 split for "clear majority" to be perceived.

Levy dug deeper into this matter by making the issue under question one that actively engaged the judges either pro or con. That is, both pro- and anti-fraternity judges were asked to decide how big a difference from 20–20 on the issue of permitting fraternities on a campus would be decisive. He found no differences in judgment as the result of the *direction* on the judge's prior commitment, suggesting that an individual in a situation where the tide of sentiment is running against him appears to perceive this just as readily as does the individual running with the tide.

Still, commitment, *per se* (regardless of its direction pro or con), *does* affect the size of difference needed for perception of a majority: When a person is

* L. H. Levy. *Percept. mot. Skills,* 1960, 11, 233–242.

committed pro *or* con it takes a greater change from a 50–50 split before he sees a majority than when the issue is an abstract one outside his interests.

In this light, a political leader or group chairman may need to be rather careful in judging voice votes or a showing of hands. There may be resistance to decisions based on less of a majority than is needed to meet the consistent and shared expectation of what constitutes a majority. Voters also prove harder to fool once they recognize that they share a common assumption about what is needed to achieve a majority.

There is some doubt about how constant in quantity the ratio is which defines a majority,* but the main point here for us is that the way has been opened for the quantitative study of a fascinating and complex problem of social perception.

PERCEPTION AND CONCEPTUALIZATION

Social perception is such a basic research topic in social psychology that we have only been able to touch on a few of the fascinating and difficult questions involved. We have seen, however, that our various everyday judgments are determined in differing degrees by a) the immediate information available to us in a situation, b) our assumptions, or habits of judgments, and c) our commitments. We have tended here to emphasize the first of these factors, both because it has often been overlooked in social psychology, and because we are beginning to learn to undertake studies and experiments on it.

But there is another reason for our present emphasis: We are interested in the relationship between social perception and social thinking. The latter grows out of the former, at least to some extent, and our thinking about social events is sometimes limited by the adequacy of our habits of attention to immediate information. Direct and repeated *attention* to complex events is one way we develop our lasting concepts and beliefs about matters social, in the sense that we learn to perceive more finely and (sometimes) with more flexibility the information that is immediately available. Julian Hochberg † has clearly shown that under limited laboratory and classroom conditions *attending behavior* can be predicted and controlled through manipulation of the forms and amounts of immediate information available to the eye. We must also learn much more about how attending sharpens our perceptual habits and provides a basis for our rich (and often confused) social concepts.

Direct, repeated attending is, of course, only one route to forming our concepts and assumptions about social events. We also pick up concepts and stereotypes indirectly. One important tradition in social psychology has

* J. R. Braun and G. A. Haven. *Percept. mot. Skills,* 1962, 14, 282.
† J. Hochberg. *Aud.-Vis. Communic. Rev.,* 1962, Vol. 10, No. 5, 49–51.

emphasized this indirect route to concepts and assumptions. Students of George Herbert Mead * have made a great deal of his idea that there is a basic, even instinctual process whereby we "take the role of the other" when we interact with people and that we thereby learn generally shared social roles indirectly without much first-hand experience. Little new learning is required for a motorist to interact accurately (that is, in the way he is *expected* to act) with a highway patrolman for the first time since the motorist has long since learned the role of the policeman and of the "caught speeder" as part of his general learning of his language and other aspects of his general culture. Our motorist simply finds himself taking the role of the *particular* policeman in a particular situation in order to infer the finer texture of the policeman's present motives and intentions. To do so he utilizes the kinds of immediate information we have emphasized above. To take the role of the other is to be able to behave (at least covertly) like the other, thereby to anticipate his probable next moves, and, above all, to do this behaving from the perspective or point of view of the other. We shall return to this idea of role and to this fascinating picture of the core process of role-taking. Our main point here is to put the spotlight on *indirect* sources of social ideas and judgments.

Ragnar Rommetveit † of Norway has done research on what he considers the three main stages in developing social concepts through *direct* experience. Consider a young lady who arrives in Paris to learn the fashion in women's clothes. She goes to salons with her knowledgeable friends and tries on clothing. Her friends, who have (in some sense) the concept of "what is fashionable," tell her when the things she tries out are fitting to the mode and when they are not. Our neophyte slowly begins to grasp the concept in a primitive sense: She can discriminate the clothes from one another more precisely than she once could, though she cannot yet pick the fitting ones from the others, nor can she state clearly at all what makes them "fitting," or *de rigeur*. She has merely learned to tell the objects one from the other more sensitively.

The second stage occurs when our visitor, through differential social rewards (her friends' agreements, the lingering eyes of men who see her pass, subtle criticisms when she buys unwisely, and all that) learns what to buy and what not to buy. She can "smell" out the fitting thing, and choose and judge what is correct. To Rommetveit, she has learned an instrumental, or useful, concept, even though she cannot yet express it verbally.

The final stage, or type, of concept attainment occurs when our heroine is able to write home and make general and accurate statements about what the fashion is. She now can describe some of the complexities of the pattern of hem height, sleeve design, and hip fitting that are, in fact, the very bases

* A. Strauss (ed.). *The social psychology of George Herbert Mead.* Chicago: University of Chicago Press, 1956.

† R. Rommetveit. Dittoed material. For related work, see *Selectivity, intuition and halo effects in social perception.* Oslo, Norway: Oslo University Press, 1960.

on which she and her (possibly inarticulate) friends are judging the social fact of "the fashion this year." This third way of having the concept is valuable indeed, and far more rare than we often think.

We have used the light-hearted domain of fashion for our example, but Rommetveit believes that this is the natural sequence of events in the direct attainment of most of our concepts. Consider the concepts of "democratic action" and "courageous action." Many people try to teach students these notions in the classroom, and this task is often attempted at the third or verbal, reporting level, skipping the earlier stages. The result may be that the student learns all the verbal statements properly associated with, say, the term "democracy," but never achieves the sensitivity to social events called for in stage one, the instrumental discriminative ability called for in stage two, or the accurate fitting of verbal descriptions to the *informational* referent in everyday life for "democracy" to make accurate use of the term.

But there is more to the story than this, if Rommetveit is correct. He points to some fascinating inconsistencies in the levels at which we hold and use concepts. In one study he found subjects who reported both before and after a sequence of experiments that they always chose their friends on the basis of "honesty," yet when actually faced with making friendship choices in the experiment, they chose potential friends for what could only be called "intellectual ability." Perhaps like the subjects we all often entertain one notion about our action at the verbal level ("I chose my friends on their honesty") while we utilize a very different concept at the level of instrumental action (choosing intelligent friends regardless of their honesty). It may be that to admit we are intellectual snobs would cause us more anxiety than we can bear, so we forget or suppress this knowledge of our actions and build our self-image around more acceptable concepts like honesty even when we fail to act on them. Many personality defenses may lie between the concepts we hold for our self-image, and those we utilize in actually making choices. Further research in this area may point up these inconsistencies and show us how to achieve more self-honesty and along with it more integrated personalities.

THE PERCEPTION OF SOCIAL ROLES

Let us return to the concept of social role that is so fashionable in contemporary sociological analysis. Social organizations can be analyzed into roles that are played, or fulfilled, by individuals who are usually replaceable. Pitchers pitch baseballs, batters aim bats at what pitchers pitch. People who pitch also bat. Batters try to play the role of pitchers in order to anticipate the form of the next pitch, as pitchers try to anticipate events from the perspective of the batter, and so on. Of course the traits, moods, and attitudes of actors help create great individual differences in the way roles are played, but over-all role structure is largely invariant, regardless of individuals.

Edgar Borgatta * has made this point clearly. He asked shy persons and forward persons to play the roles of both a shy policeman and a dominant policeman in a small group. The dominant persons played less shy "shy policemen" than did the shy persons, and the shy persons produced less dominant "dominant policemen" than did the dominant ones. But neither group had trouble in producing behavior appropriate to the given roles.

No doubt we all learn to judge the appropriateness of the behaviors of people who play many common roles around us. We all feel quite assured in saying, "He's not acting like a proper policeman, or Senator, or liberal." Further, we are apparently able to discriminate even the more subtle roles, as when we look to the high producer in a group for leadership in getting a job done, but turn to a different person when we have a gripe, or need to be reassured. We may not even have terms for such a difference in role (say, "task leader" vs. "emotional leader") since the concepts underlying our different behavior toward them have not developed to Rommetveit's third (accurately articulate) stage. Yet we are even able to spot the apparent effects of a role that have rubbed off on a person even when he is not actually "in the role." A retired general is often palpably a general still, and a policeman on vacation often gives himself away, not only by owning big feet, but by the things he pays attention to or his special knowledge of city hall politics or other matters that are not even necessarily directly tied to his usual role.

The perception of roles and role effects is a complex and sophisticated case of social perception. In a sense it represents an integration of all the processes discussed in this chapter. Our assumptions about a person in a role cover his feelings and his emotional expressions ("a diplomat should at least appear to be cool and collected"); his motivations and traits ("Caesar's wife should be virtuous, or at least send information to that effect"); his intentions ("a good cop should be helpful to kids, or at least make the kids think he is"); his contributing to a social situation ("a good Senator suggests new laws"); and his position in a social hierarchy ("politicians are big shots in our town"). All these (and many other as yet unstudied) facts of social perception will help cast light on role perception, which is so related to accurate social behavior. The more intimate, lengthy, and important our interaction with others, the more differentiated and accurate our role judgments become, so that more aspects of the other person, his performance, and the situational setting become relevant.

A role is, then, a complex entity, and recently social psychologists have become interested in the principles by which people master the complexity of role judgment. How do the parts coalesce into a unified role impression? Harry Triandis and Martin Fishbein * have concentrated on how beliefs and

* E. Borgatta. "Role specification and personality" (mimeographed report, 1961), Cornell University.

† H. C. Triandis and M. Fishbein. "Cognitive interaction in person perception." *J. abnorm. soc. Psychol.*, Fall, 1963, 2–29.

evaluations of separate "role terms" determine the final evaluation of a cluster of these terms. Knowing a subject's beliefs and evaluations about Negroes and coal miners, the problem is to predict how he will evaluate the description "a Negro coal miner." This is a fairly simple task. The technical difficulty is greater, of course, when we attempt to predict from knowledge about the various components the resultant evaluation of "Negro Portuguese coal miner of different religion from yours."

Evaluations and beliefs of the part as predictors of the evaluation of the total tap only a limited segment of role perception. There is more to perception than the judgment of value, but such judgment is certainly relevant.

Consider a subject who likes Negroes but hates coal miners. The most fashionable theories in social psychology—those called balance, or consistency, theories—would all predict that he would evaluate a "Negro coal miner" somewhere on a scale *between* his liking for Negroes and his dislike for coal miners. Such a resolution would provide more balance in his thoughts than would either of the extremes, and would provide the congruity people prefer as against the incongruity arising from the two incompatible terms.

Using role descriptions, Triandis and Fishbein analyzed the judgments of a number of subjects from both Greece and the United States. They found at once that for both Greeks and Americans the *occupational component* in such a role description as "Negro Portuguese coal miner of a different religion from yours" is the most powerful component in forming the total judgment. The next most important component for the Greeks was religion; for the Americans it was race.

Theoretically, however, their most interesting discovery was that the balance notion, though it predicted the judgment of the composites fairly well, did not do so well as what they call the cognitive summation principle. Whereas in the balance theories the value of the complex role is related to the *mean*, or *average*, of the scaled value of the components, in the alternative theory the composite judgment is related to the *sum*, or *total*, of the scaled value contributions of each of the components, weighted, of course (as in the case of the occupational component above), by their prominence. Whereas under balance theories two liked things, when put together, would never be evaluated higher than the more liked of the two, in Fishbein's theory two well-liked things, put together, could produce a composite that is even more liked than either of the components. The whole, in short, is more like the sum of the values of the parts than like some point *in between* the values of the parts.

IN PERSPECTIVE

This chapter has documented how our accurate perceptual behavior *vis-à-vis* social events rests upon the information about the event that is immediately available. Related to, and usually aroused by, such immediate cues, however, are more or less complex associational and cognitive *mediators*, such as cultural codes, that help to interpret the information provided by the social event itself. Thus, there are invariant relationships between eye and head placement that are related to the judgment of being looked at; there are three dimensions of judgment that help to order the information from other people's faces and thus "place" their emotion; a more or less complex set of assumptions helps us to sort out other people's decisions in making choices so that we can arrive at judgments of their intentions; when someone agrees with us we assess the cause according to our judgment of his relative status, assigning the agreement to *him* if he is above us, and to *our* arguments if he is below us; we are influenced by the usual activeness of others in giving out credit for social contributions; many situations are perceived with the aid of our personal or socially shared concepts of what is expected of a person in a role; we tend to assume that hierarchies of people are ordered simply until we learn otherwise (if we ever do).

The study of social perception has been held back by the technical troubles that arise when we try to systematically vary the occurrence of social events, but a start has been made. A study of the issues involved in the intercommunication of social and personal cues, along with conditions for the reception of such cues, is also underway.

The problem of the perception of persons in roles and the question of how the observer integrates the complex evaluational and other information involved in such an act has been pointed up as a central issue in the study of the perception of social events.

The Social Significance
of Attitudes

Suppose you were asked to look carefully at a picture of two men standing in a subway train, one of them a Negro, the other a white man. The white man is holding, of all things, an open straight-edge razor in his hand. Then suppose you were to describe the picture, in as much detail as possible, to another person who did not actually see it himself, so that he could relate its contents to someone else, and so on through five or six others. What would happen to the message as it passed through this human chain? Research with American students has shown * that if you and the other members of the group were white, and

* See Otto Klineberg. *Social psychology*. New York: Holt, 1954, chapter 8.

4

under 10 years of age, the details of the picture would get through with only slight errors of memory. But if you and your group were in your teens or older, the basic facts would very likely be distorted: the razor would have "moved," somewhere along the transmission chain, to the Negro's hand, and he would likely be described as "threatening" the white man! What causes these distortions of perception and memory?

In another community, Protestant children were asked "What do you think Jews are like?" and their responses were analyzed for prejudice.* At 5 years of age, none expressed prejudice or discrimination in their replies, while at 10 years 27 per cent did. And by the age of 10, the children were clearly showing discrimination by excluding Jewish children from their groups of friends. The same development was noted in other large American cities †: Starting in the fifth grade, but not before, children of Italian background typically choose other Italians and Jewish children choose other Jews as friends. What mediates these predictable changes in perspectives of others as children grow older?

In this chapter we keep our sights fixed on the fine texture of social behavior, on the ways human beings adjust to their social world. But here we focus sharply on one very special form of adjustment—the development of attitudes. The study of attitudes has become a major concern of social psychologists over the years because it is a complex psychological phenomenon that has tremendous social significance.

The examples just given touch on the development of prejudiced attitudes. Throughout this chapter we shall use prejudice as one of the principal examples of attitudes for two reasons: because its social significance has prompted a great deal of theory and research to draw on; and because prejudice highlights the essential components found in all types of attitudes. Our chapter plan is, first, to define what we mean by "attitudes" and describe their general characteristics, and, second, to demonstrate with specific research examples how attitudes are measured. Then we shall illustrate how attitudes affect our behavior and personalities. Finally, we shall explain (as well as we can with the facts now known) how attitudes are formed—that is, how they are learned—and how they can be changed.

THE NATURE OF ATTITUDES

An attitude is an organized and consistent manner of thinking, feeling, and reacting with regard to people, groups, social issues, or, more generally, any event in one's environment. Its essential components are thoughts and beliefs, feelings (or emotions), and tendencies to react. We say that an attitude is formed when these components are so interrelated that specific feelings and

* Margaret Birks. Discrimination among Jewish and Protestant children. Unpublished M.A. Thesis. Redpath Library, McGill University, 1957.
† See J. H. Criswell. *Archives of Psychol.*, 1939, No. 235.

reaction tendencies become consistently associated with a particular way of thinking about certain persons or events. We develop our attitudes in the process of coping with and adjusting to our social environments, and, once developed, they lend regularity to our modes of reacting and facilitate social adjustment. In the early stages of the development of an attitude, its components are not so rigidly systematized that they cannot be modified by new experiences. But later their organization can become inflexible and stereotyped, especially for those persons who have been encouraged over long periods of time to react in standard or "acceptable" ways to particular events or groups. If a person's attitudes become firmly set, he is then too ready to categorize people or events into one of his emotionally toned patterns of thoughts so that he fails to either examine or recognize their individuality. It is in this fashion that fixed or stereotyped attitudes reduce the potential richness of a person's environment and constrict his reactions to it.

We are not fully conscious of most of our attitudes nor are we aware of the extensive influence they have on our social behavior. But on very close self-analysis, we can detect the functioning of certain attitudes within ourselves. For example, if a person has developed a strong negative attitude towards communism, say, he considers and evaluates any action by communists in a stereotyped fashion. If he examines himself carefully, he can actually sense his reactions of suspicion or hatred as he reads or hears about their activities. Similarly, when a new acquaintance turns out to have the same views as we do toward various social issues, we sense a closeness and attraction as the favorable attitude toward him develops.

Through introspective glimpses of attitudes functioning within ourselves, we become sensitive to the attitudes of others. But people do not always openly reveal their attitudes. In fact, they learn through experiences with others to keep certain of their attitudes hidden from casual acquaintances, or even from close friends. With this in mind, we have used the term "reaction tendency" rather than "reaction" for the third component of attitudes in order to indicate that they are not necessarily expressed in overt behavior. And because this is so, success in social interaction often turns on skill at inferring the nature of others' thoughts, feelings, and reaction tendencies from very subtle behavioral cues. Actually, it is a common characteristic of human thought to make inferences about the attitudes of others and to regulate one's own actions accordingly. From small and limited samples of another's behavior we may conclude, say, that he is liberal, understanding, or unprejudiced, and then react to him in what we consider to be an appropriate manner. But though we all make such inferences, people differ in their capacity to make them correctly. The socially sensitive person has a good deal of this skill. In fact, he can be so sensitive to the attitudes of others that he is socially incapacitated. On the other hand, the socially clumsy person frequently misses or misinterprets the available cues. In many instances this type of individual habitually makes incorrect inferences about another's attitudes because his own get in the way. That is, he may incorrectly assume that others share his prejudices, having convinced himself that his views are the only logical ones. But even the socially clumsy person can learn to recognize the consistency of another's ways of reacting and make reliable inferences about attitudes. He can, for example, profit from his experiences with close friends who are often able to freely discuss their differences of thoughts and feelings about mutually important subjects and thereby learn how to make more accurate inferences about each other's attitudes.

THE MEASUREMENT OF ATTITUDES

Social psychologists have developed a number of systematic techniques for inferring and measuring attitudes. If a measuring instrument is to be useful, it must, of course, reliably register variations in quantities of some sort so that the measured elements can be compared and placed in an order. Devices to measure attitudes, like other instruments, are tested and reworked until they reliably reflect degrees of favorable or unfavorable attitudes. Special problems, however, crop up with such psychological measuring devices: People and their attitudes are not necessarily the same from one time period to another, so it is more difficult to determine a device's reliability than is the case with physical measurement. Furthermore, it is not possible to make direct measurements of complex psychological processes such as attitudes. When asked to express or discuss their attitudes, most people give incomplete, superficial, and often distorted descriptions of them. Therefore, psychologists must infer their existence and characteristics from information available about individuals' thoughts, feelings, and reaction tendencies. Because attitudes can not be directly measured, the indirect inferences made about them require careful testing for validity—that is, it must be established that attitude measures actually measure what they are supposed to and not some other psychological process.

Information needed for inferring attitudes can be obtained by observing people in specially created social situations. Because such an approach takes a great deal of time and is unnatural for those being observed, psychologists have developed substitute procedures. In the typical case, respondents are asked to imagine themselves in certain social situations and provide information concerning their thoughts, feelings, and likely ways of behaving in such settings. For example, Emory Bogardus * asked subjects to imagine themselves in various types of social contact with foreigners, say, Chinese people, and to indicate whether they would like to have them as very close friends, as neighbors, as colleagues at work, and so forth. The situations ranged in scaled steps from acceptance as a marriage partner to rejection even as visitors to one's country. Bogardus' "social distance scale" permitted an ordering of respondents in terms of their reaction tendencies; thus, some

* E. S. Bogardus. *J. appl. Sociol.*, 1925, 9, 299–308.

would **agree** to accept Chinese as neighbors, while others, showing less desire for social distance, would accept Chinese as potential close friends or marriage partners. (Whether respondents would do so in actual social contexts would depend on the permissiveness of the setting itself and the intensity of their reaction tendencies.) The Bogardus scale has been a useful instrument in attitude research, in spite of these limitations: It doesn't provide an index of degree or intensity of reaction tendencies, nor does it obtain information about the thoughts and feelings of respondents. Techniques developed more recently probe into all three aspects of attitudes and insure that variations in the intensity of thoughts, feelings, and reaction tendencies can be measured.

Let us follow through a typical example of how social psychologists go about measuring attitudes. Suppose we were interested in determining the attitudes of Americans towards recent immigrants. We might plan the study so that communities of different size could be compared, working on the hunch that residents of large cities would be less sensitive than those in small communities to the presence of immigrants. We might also argue in advance that sensitivity towards immigrants would be particularly evident in those who risk losing their jobs to new competition, or in those who live in neighborhoods the immigrants would most likely move into. Questions about these matters could be answered by selecting representative samples or respondents from different socio-economic backgrounds and from different neighborhoods in each community to be studied. At a more personal level, we might anticipate that those with unfavorable attitudes towards immigrants might have a general trait of ethnocentrism. In order to have information to test such an idea, of course, we would have to include ways of measuring ethnocentrism and generalized prejudice in the research plans.

Suppose we decided to use a questionnaire method for measuring attitudes towards immigrants, and to make comparisons of type (favorable or unfavorable) and degree of attitude the major interests. Questionnaire items would then be constructed to represent the three components of attitudes. Respondents would get the opportunity to agree or disagree with each question, thus indicating type of attitude; the *intensity* of response would be reflected in whether they say they agree strongly, agree, are uncertain, disagree, or strongly disagree. For example, the questions "Generally speaking, I believe immigrants are as trustworthy as anyone else" and "Immigrants seem to have children primarily to send them out to work" permit respondents to express their *thoughts* and *beliefs* about immigrants. The questions "It bothers me the way immigrants stick to their own language and customs" and "I am happy to have my children play with immigrant children" allow expression of *feelings* and *emotions* with regard to immigrants. The questions "I would be quite willing to work for an immigrant employer" and "I would likely move out if too many immigrants took homes in my district" allow expression of *reaction tendencies*. If several questions were devised to measure each attitude component, then the *consistency* of the organization of components could be assessed. Furthermore, if half the questions were favorably worded and half unfavorably, we could determine whether an attitude was actually being expressed (in which case, respondents would agree with the questions in one form and disagree with those in the opposite form) or a tendency to comply revealed (that is, indiscriminately agreeing with any statements, favorable or not).

We would first administer the questionnaire on two different occasions to a test group of representative respondents in order to determine its *reliability*: It would be reliable to the extent that the questions elicited the same responses on both occasions. We would then eliminate questions that proved unreliable. We could examine the *validity* of the questionnaire in numerous ways. For example, a panel of foremen in an industry could give us the names of workers who were known to be friendly with immigrant workers and the names of those who had shown hostility to immigrants at work. The questionnaire would be valid to the extent that the friendly and the hostile subgroups could be easily distinguished by total scores derived from responses to all questions. We could also assess the value of each question by certain technical procedures (which we needn't go into here) so that we could eliminate redundant questions or those that did not contribute to the effectiveness of the total questionnaire in discriminating among types of attitude. When acceptable limits of reliability, validity, and item-value have been met, the questionnaire would become a powerful research tool for discovering the social and psychological significance of attitudes.

We shall examine the usefulness of questionnaire techniques in the next section and we shall also describe other methods of inferring attitudes that rely less on the cooperation of subjects. The aim of these alternative methods is to devise special experimental situations in such a fashion that subjects are not aware that they reveal their private thoughts, feelings, and reaction tendencies.

THE FUNCTION OF ATTITUDES

Attitudes play an essential role in determining our behavior; for example, they affect our judgments and perceptions of others, they influence our speed and efficiency of learning, they help determine the groups we associate with, the professions we finally choose, and even the philosophies we live by. We shall use four research examples here to demonstrate just how attitudes do affect behavior. In the first two, the researchers were more interested in how groups of people, rather than individuals, behave. Instead of measuring each subject's attitudes, they presumed that the majority of the members of the groups studied held stereotyped attitudes and that, if the presumption was correct, the groups should behave in predictable fashions because of these prevalent attitudes. In the third and fourth examples, variations in the type and degree of an individual's attitudes were of prime interest, and measurements of these variations were made by questionnaire techniques.

The first study * we shall examine was carried out in Montreal, a community whose history reveals a French-English schism that is perhaps as socially significant for residents of the Province of Quebec as that between the North and South is for Southerners in the United States. The purpose of the study was to determine how French- and English-speaking Montrealers view one another. Since members of both cultural groups are identified by the language they speak, the researchers decided to use the spoken language as a means of eliciting stereotyped attitudes. In the first part of the study English-Canadian college students listened to the recorded voices of English and French speakers (all reading versions of the same passage) and indicated on check-lists what they thought the personality traits of the speakers were. The students were told that the task was like guessing the characteristics of a person heard on the phone for the first time. They listened to and judged the personalities of ten speakers, and even though some spoke in French, they were told to disregard language and to concentrate on voice and personality in making their ratings. The students were *not* told that in reality they were to hear the voices of five perfectly bilingual speakers, reading once in English and once in Canadian-style French.

With this procedure, obviously, it would be very difficult for the students to disregard the language spoken; any differences in their personality judgments of the French and English guises of the *same* speakers would likely be attributable to stereotyped attitudes they had developed toward members of the two cultural groups. As it turned out, the English guises of the speakers were more favorably evaluated on a series of traits than were the French guises of the same speakers. For example, the English-Canadian judges perceived the English guises as being better looking, taller, more intelligent, more dependable, kinder, more ambitious, and of better character than the French. In only one trait were the French guises viewed more favorably—sense of humor.

In the second part of the study, French-Canadian college students were given the same test. It is of particular interest that they, too, evaluated the *English* guises of the speakers significantly *more* favorably than the French ones on good looks, height, leadership, intelligence, self-confidence, dependability, ambition, sociability, character, and likeableness. This result indicates that many young French-Canadians regard their cultural group as an inferior one. Inferiority of this sort is in fact evident among Canadian bilinguals, who often comment that they sense they are better received by both groups when speaking English. They themselves feel more important, as though they were considered more valuable by their social audiences, when they use English.

* W. E. Lambert, R. C. Hodgson, R. C. Gardner, and S. Fillenbaum. *J. abnorm. soc. Psychol.*, 1960, 60, 44–51.

The reactions of the French-Canadian students, then, demonstrate that the attitudes of members of a minority group are affected by contacts with groups that are perceived to have higher social status. This tendency has been noted by other researchers in quite different social settings. For example, in communities where they are viewed as inferior by the majority groups, Jews adopt some of the anti-Semitic beliefs and Negroes take on anti-Negro attitudes. To better their status and enhance their sense of worth, members of minority groups apparently identify with and unwittingly incorporate the stereotyped or prejudiced attitudes of those with power.

Cultural and linguistic changes will likely take place along such sensitive seams of inferiority. For example, French-Canadian leaders may become aware of the implications of this sense of inferiority and try to eradicate it by stressing the distinctive values of their own culture. Or the attitude of inferiority could spread through the French-Canadian community, increasing the tendency to learn and use English and decreasing the desire of French children to use French. The case is analogous to that of immigrants who try to get rid of their foreign customs and languages as rapidly as possible because they realize that the social judgments of members of the established group are often colored by stereotyped ethnocentric attitudes.

Attitudes and the Reaction to Pain

In this next study,* college students who volunteered to be subjects in an investigation of pain had their "pain tolerance levels" measured by means of a slightly modified sphygmomanometer—the gadget used to determine blood pressure. The instrument was modified by sewing a set of pointed, hard-rubber projections into the pressure cuff. With the cuff wrapped around a subject's upper arm, the examiner increased the air pressure, forcing the sharp projections into the arm, until the subject said he could no longer tolerate the pain. The experimenter then released the pressure and told the subject that a second measure would be taken a minute or so later to establish the reliability of the tolerance threshold just measured. There was no way for the subjects to know about the actual design of the study: that they had been chosen on the basis of their religion—half were Christian and half were Jewish—and that they were to be induced to grit their teeth and really suffer as certain attitudes were brought into play.

While waiting between sessions, the subjects spontaneously asked for more details about the undertaking. To Christians, the experimenter explained that certain reported research indicated Christians could not tolerate as much pain as Jews; the purpose of the study, he said, was to check on this claim. Jewish students were told just the opposite. Thus, both groups of students were led to believe that they could enhance the reputation of their own religious groups if they took more pain on the second trial. The

* W. E. Lambert, Eva Libman, and E. G. Poser. *J. Pers.,* 1960, 28, 350–357.

amount of suffering endured would depend, then, on their attitudes of allegiance to their religious groups. On the second trial, both the Jewish and Christian subjects took significantly more pain, in many cases so much more that deep impressions of the hard projections remained on their arms for several minutes. The behavior of both groups was clearly modified by the fictitious information given them. And yet, it was not clear whether each group was trying to beat out the other by being tougher, or whether each was merely trying to come in line, so as not to appear different from the other group. (Control subjects, those receiving no information during the waiting period, took essentially the same amount of pain on both trials.) To examine this possibility, other groups of Christian and Jewish students were tested in the same manner except that during the waiting period they were informed that their religious group purportedly could tolerate *more* pain than the other. There were several possible outcomes. If, for example, the Jewish subjects were anxious to be more like the Christians, they might reduce the amount of pain taken on the second trial. Or they could take more and thereby reveal that they wanted to surpass the norm of the Christians. On the second trial, the Christians took more pain even after learning that Christians had the higher tolerance level. They acted as though they wanted to extend their lead or to dissociate themselves as far as possible from Jews in this regard. The Jewish subjects in contrast held their own: They neither increased nor decreased their tolerance level. Apparently they were interested either in eliminating any differences in toughness that might exist between their religious group and Christians or in maintaining any superiority they may have had in this regard. As the over-all findings highlight, behavior can be dramatically modified when appropriate attitudes are aroused.

Attitudes and Learning

If you were asked to **learn**
a series of arguments supporting a point of view that you didn't believe in at all, would your attitudes get in the way and make it difficult for you to assimilate the new ideas? In the experiments we are considering here,* this question was put to test, and the answer, it turns out, is more complex than one might at first think. The topic at issue was segregation. Two groups of white college students in the South were selected to be subjects: one clearly prosegregation, the other antisegregation in attitudes, as measured by a specially devised questionnaire. Both groups were asked to learn thoroughly 11 brief statements arguing against segregation. They were to remember especially the core ideas presented in each statement, much as one would learn a series of legal principles from a textbook on law in preparation for an examination. The statements were of this type: "The issue of Negro-White integrated education has nothing to do with racial intermarriage"; or "The

* E. E. Jones and Jane Aneshansel. *J. abnorm. soc. Psychol.*, 1956, 53, 27–33; E. E. Jones and Rika Kohler. *J. abnorm. soc. Psychol.*, 1958, 57, 315–320.

Negro points up the greatest disparity between the theory and our practice of democracy." Each subject read the 11 statements aloud, one at a time, and then tried to reproduce as many as possible from memory. He went through this procedure five times and his efficiency of recall was determined for each trial. Note that those with attitudes favoring segregation were asked to learn arguments that were "contravaluent," that is, directly opposite to their own point of view, whereas the antisegregationists were learning material congruent with their attitudes.

The results of the experiment were clear: Students who were against segregation learned the antisegregation arguments more efficiently than did those who favored segregation. In other words, material that was congenial with existing attitudes was more readily assimilated. Apparently, the attitudes functioned as a type of filter, letting congenial ideas enter into memory easily, but stopping or distorting the meaning of ideas that ran counter to personal values.

Then the researchers asked themselves another question. If students were informed that they were to make further use of these arguments—for example, to use them as a rebuttal in a debate—would they still learn better the congenial arguments? To test this notion, two other groups of students, one prosegregation and one antisegregation, were told in advance that they were to learn the statements in order to use them later as counterarguments when *prosegregation* statements would be presented to them. That is, they were informed that the learning task would help them later on to destroy arguments supporting segregation, and that they would be examined for their skill in using the arguments they were to learn. In this case, it was found that prosegregationists learned the antisegregation arguments *more* efficiently than did the antisegregationists. In other words, students with favorable attitudes toward segregation apparently became particularly attentive to the antisegregation arguments because it was necessary to know these contravaluent ideas well in order to use them in the rebuttal to follow. The antisegregation arguments apparently passed too easily through the filtering systems of the antisegregationists. They had deluded themselves that they thoroughly understood these ideas.

In an extension of this experiment, Edward Jones and Rika Kohler wondered whether attitudes would affect the efficiency of learning in the same way if the arguments to be learned were congenial but not logically convincing. To test this idea they selected, as before, students with prosegregation and antisegregation attitudes and presented them with 12 statements to learn. In this case, six of the statements were prosegregation in content and six were antisegregation, and within each group of six, three were "implausible" or based on illogical premises (for instance, "If Negroes and whites were meant to live together, they never would have been separated at the beginning of history"), and three were "plausible" (for instance, "Southerners will have to pay the price of lowered scholastic standards if they yield to the pressures to integrate their schools"). The results demonstrated very convincingly that *both* groups of students learned better those statements that were congruent with their attitudes *if* they were plausible. However, they learned the *contravaluent* statements better when they were implausible. These findings indicate that individuals protect their values and attitudes by bulwarking them with good supportive arguments and by enhancing the unreasonableness of the opposing points of view.

Attitudes and On-the-job Productivity

There are intriguing cases in psychological research where a particular attitude, once believed to play a critical role in certain behavior—so much so that a whole national movement developed to cultivate the "proper" attitude—was revealed by later examination to have little or no connection with the behavior in question. One example we particularly have in mind here is the assumption held by many industrial managers that workers with favorable attitudes toward their jobs will be especially productive. Largely on their faith in this proposition, American industrial leaders "humanized" their relations with workers to insure that attitudes towards working conditions would be favorable.

In 1955, Arthur Brayfield and Walter Crockett * analyzed the host of studies carried out in industries during the past 40 years on the relationship between the attitudes of employees (measured by questionnaires, rating scales, or interviews) and their on-the-job productivity. The conclusions are instructive: There is little if any evidence that an employee's attitudes toward his work bears any relation to his productivity. In other words, high producers are as often dissatisfied as they are satisfied with their working conditions. Industrialists had apparently made a wrong guess about the attitudes of workers and about the goals they strive for. Brayfield and Crockett point out that the error came in presuming that productivity was necessarily as important a goal for workers as it may be for those at managerial levels. Workers may not be as oriented toward achievement as middle-class managers may inaccurately presume from a consideration of their own inclinations. For the worker, productivity is more likely a means to the attainment of other goals, rather than an end in itself.

When basic needs for personal and family comfort are met, most workers look toward social goals, aims such as being liked by others or feeling a part of social groups. In their view, overproduction might bring on the wrath of coworkers and union officials who would feel threatened by a "rate-buster." So workers who are satisfied with their conditions might regulate their rate of production so as *not* to get raises or advancements since such prizes might lead to their being drawn out of comfortable cliques both inside and outside the plant. Conversely, those who are dissatisfied with their working conditions might produce at a fast clip in order to move out of what to them is an uncomfortable environment. The point here is that although workers' atti-

* A. H. Brayfield and W. H. Crockett. *Psychol. Bull.*, 1955, 52, 396–424.

tudes towards issues they consider important certainly do affect their working habits, including productivity, the relationship between attitudes and work is more complex than was at first presumed by those industrial managers who, extending their own attitudes, misjudged the feelings, desires, and goals of workers.

Attitudes and Personality

To illustrate how attitudes affect various forms of behavior, we have just examined several research examples, each concerned with the actions of a different group of subjects. In this section, we are interested in another feature of attitudes: how, for the same person or group of people, they become interrelated and organized, or in other words, how attitudes give form and structure to personalities. In the illustrations given above, we had glimpses of this interrelationship. Workers, for one instance, apparently have an organized pattern of attitudes towards their work, bosses, colleagues, and off-the-job friends. For another, the white students in the South who were against segregation would likely be sympathetic towards various minority groups. We would expect to find patterns of tolerant or prejudiced attitudes of this sort because other social-psychological research has established that people with friendly (or hostile) attitudes toward certain minority or foreign groups tend to be friendly (or hostile) toward all such groups. This finding suggests that tolerance and prejudice are more than learned ways of reacting to specific groups; they are more likely generalized personality traits.

The possibility that attitudes are basic features of personality was examined further in a recent study of the attitudes of minority-group members.* The investigators measured the attitudes of Jewish high school students towards both Gentiles and Jews. In this case, too, they noted that anti-Gentile and anti-Jewish attitudes were highly correlated—that is, those students who were most tolerant of Gentiles were also most tolerant of their own group and those who disliked one group disliked the other. Each of these students was also examined for attitudes toward self, attitudes towards parents, and general tendencies to be hostile. When the researchers examined all these factors, they observed that students with marked hostility tendencies revealed an antagonistic personality trait: They held unfavorable attitudes toward their parents, toward members of the majority group, and toward members of their own religious group. Students with favorable attitudes toward both religious groups also had favorable attitudes toward self and parents—that is, they had friendly and tolerant dispositions.

In one of the most comprehensive studies ever undertaken of the interrelationships of attitudes,† investigators found that prejudiced attitudes pattern themselves in a rather dramatic fashion. Ethnocentrism, attitudes towards

* M. Anisfield, et al. J. abnorm. soc. Psychol., 1963, 66, 31–36.

† T. W. Adorno, et al. The authoritarian personality. New York: Harper, 1950.

Negroes, degree of patriotism, political conservatism, and attitudes towards Jews all correlated, presenting the picture of the prejudiced person (in contrast to the unprejudiced) as anti-Jewish, anti-Negro, anti-foreign groups in general, overly and uncritically patriotic, and extremely conservative in political outlook. Although more research on this topic is called for, such studies are nevertheless impressive for the emergence of general personality dispositions composed of patterns of attitudes—an open friendliness toward others versus a sour negativeness, for example, or a democratic versus an antidemocratic outlook. Future research will undoubtedly discover various clusters of attitudes and explain their development. Even now, though, we realize that the attitudes we develop form consistent patterns and that these attitude networks contribute to the structure of our personalities.

THE DEVELOPMENT OF ATTITUDES

In our definition of attitudes, we emphasized that they are "organized," "consistent," and "habitual" ways of thinking, feeling, and reacting with regard to events and persons in one's environment. We used these adjectives to indicate that attitudes are learned modes of adjustment, that is, complex habits. Their development, therefore, should follow standard principles of learning. Our purpose in this section, then, is to introduce three interrelated principles that help explain how attitudes are learned, namely the principles of *association, transfer,* and *need satisfaction.*

In general, we learn feelings and reaction tendencies, two of the components of attitudes, through *association* and *need satisfaction.* That is, we learn to fear and avoid people or things associated with unpleasant happenings, to like and approach those associated with pleasurable happenings. By avoiding in the first case and approaching in the second we satisfy basic needs for pleasure or comfort. For example, our most basic attitudes are learned in infancy through interaction with our parents. Typically, an infant develops strong favorable attitudes towards parents because, by caring for his needs and comforting him, their presence becomes associated with his contentment and general well-being. In time, as parents become associated with punishments as well as pleasures, the child's attitudes toward them will become complex and ambivalent.

An interesting recent experiment with grade school children demonstrates how attitudes towards others are learned through both association and need satisfaction.* The idea being tested was that a child develops positive attitudes toward others if, while in their presence, he is pleasantly surprised. None of the children chosen for the experiment, it should be noted, were close friends at the start of the study. The children were organized in groups of three, and each group was given an interesting game to play. During the

* Bernice E. Lott, and A. J. Lott. *J. abnorm. soc. Psychol.,* 1960, 61, 297–300.

games, children in some groups received toys as prizes; other groups received none. Some time after the games, the classroom teacher asked each child to name two children with whom he would like to spend a holiday. It turned out that those who had received prizes chose more of their fellow play-group associates as vacation friends than did those who got no toys. As predicted, positive attitudes developed towards play-group members in those cases where playing together was associated with a pleasurable event. This finding lends support to the principles underlying the study, and the principles themselves help explain how unfavorable attitudes can develop, or be intensified, in social contexts where we experience disappointments or failures in the presence of members of some distinctive group. A person's failures in school or at work, for example, can become associated with the presence of certain others who do relatively well. In such instances, unfavorable attitudes are revealed in such remarks as "How can you get ahead with so many of *them* around!" By placing the blame for his difficulties on others, he satisfies a need for self respect. In a similar fashion, positive attitudes towards members of the "old gang" with whom we have our good times can develop or strengthen. To extend the principles, members of a whole community often develop negative attitudes towards racial or immigrant groups whom they associate with their economic difficulties.

Whereas feelings and reaction tendencies toward others are commonly learned through association and need satisfaction, we typically acquire our thoughts and beliefs, the third component of attitudes, in a different fashion. In fact, attitudes learned by association and need satisfaction are often characterized, in the early stages of their development, by the learner's inability to comprehend *why* he feels and reacts as he does. This inability to comprehend makes him especially attentive to the thoughts and beliefs of others, and he may readily adopt these as a means of justifying his own feelings and reaction tendencies. Our purpose here is to introduce the principle of *transfer* which helps explain how we learn attitudes—especially the thought-belief components—from other people.

Actually we learn attitudes through transfer in essentially the same way we learn meanings of concepts through instruction. For instance, a child will immediately develop a meaning for "zebra" when told it is a "horse-like" animal with "up-and-down stripes." In this example, two unrelated ideas of the child ("horse" and "up-and-down stripes") are brought into a novel combination for the first time. In a similar fashion, our social "teachers" can transfer attitudes by suggesting how we should reorganize and integrate certain of our basic ideas. When a close relationship exists between teacher and learner, feelings and reaction tendencies can also be transferred along with thoughts and beliefs. For instance, someone could transfer a completely favorable attitude towards Negroes by describing them as "dark-skinned," "maltreated," "hardworking," "friendly," and "lively." Or he could transfer a full-blown negative attitude by describing Negroes as "dark-skinned," "lazy," "undependable," "dirty," and "untrustworthy." Although attitudes are very commonly learned through transfer, we are not often fully aware of the principle's significance until we encounter such facts as the following: In a midwestern American community that had no Jewish or Negro residents at all, anti-Semitism and prejudice toward Negroes were found to be as strong and prevalent among teen-agers as in large eastern cities heavily populated by Jews and Negroes.* In this case, the unfavorable attitudes could not have been learned through association; they were transferred.

But we don't incorporate all attitudes directed our way; that we are selective about which attitudes we pick up indicates that need satisfaction is usually involved when attitudes are transferred. As children, we are attentive to, and usually adopt the attitudes of, our parents as a normal part of becoming educated. We do so because, in being like them in this respect, we assure ourselves of their affection at the same time as we strengthen our feeling of belonging in the family. Children's needs for affection and belonging are not always satisfied in the family, of course, and they can show their hostility by failing to adopt their parents' attitudes in transfer, or by adopting contrary ones.

We also adopt attitudes of other important people outside the family. As we grow older, we incorporate attitudes that seem appropriate for belonging to groups we consider important. Sometimes we change attitudes as a means of leaving one group and becoming part of another. A study by Theodore Newcomb † demonstrates how the need-satisfaction principle works in determining attitude transfer. Newcomb made extensive examinations over a four-year period of students' attitudes and personalities in a small New England women's college. Most students came from politically and socially conservative homes, but the college faculty and advanced students had created a decidedly liberal atmosphere in the academic community. The majority of girls adopted the liberal values of the community, but a minority showed no change, some even intensifying their conservatism. By the fourth year it was evident that those who became liberal had done so both in order to obtain the approval of their fellow students and the faculty and to satisfy their need to become independent of their parents. In contrast, those who remained conservative had, apparently because of their timidity and feelings of inadequacy, psychologically withdrawn from the community and were thereby immune from influence. As a group, they kept their original attitudes either as a consequence of protecting themselves from a threatening social environment or as an attempt to maintain the affection of their parents. Thus, important social needs were satisfied for both those who adopted and those who failed to adopt new attitudes.

* Judy F. Rosenblith. *J. abnorm. soc. Psychol.,* 1949, 44, 470–489.
† T. M. Newcomb. *Personality and social change: Attitude formation in a student community.* New York: Holt, Rinehart and Winston (Dryden), 1943.

At first glance, the changing of attitudes might seem to be a simple matter. Since attitudes are learned, it should be easy enough to modify their intensity or replace an undesirable one by learning another. The complicating fact, however, is that attitudes are not as easily modified or replaced as they are learned. As we have seen, once attitudes are developed, they become integral aspects of an individual's personality, affecting his whole style of behavior. Changing them is not easy, as the Chinese captors found out when they tried to induce American soldiers to learn a new set of attitudes. Well-planned attempts to modify attitudes often succeed only in altering the thought-belief component without affecting feelings and reaction tendencies so that in time the attitude may revert to its former state. Those attitudes developed in the home or through early experiences in groups are particularly instrumental in forming the structure of attitude networks, and are especially resistant to modification. Nevertheless, we know that attitudes can be changed under certain conditions. For instance, some of the college girls we just talked about, in the process of leaving home and becoming part of a new community, demonstrably shifted from conservative to liberal attitudes, or at least the intensity of their conservatism was reduced. Far more research is needed to explain both the persistence and modifiability of attitudes. Although no final answers are available, we can anticipate that studies will reveal attitudes to be particularly resistant to change a) if they have been learned early in life, b) if they have been learned by association as well as transfer, c) if they help satisfy needs, and d) if they have been integrated into one's personality and style of behaving.

Learning and Attitude Change

Social psychologists are guided by such general rules in their attempts to change attitudes. They realize that if attitudes are to be replaced or their intensity modified, the new ideas and beliefs that are to be learned must be very skillfully presented, usually in the form of persuasive communications. If habitual modes of feeling and reacting are to be altered, actual social settings, or contrived experimental ones, must be so arranged that new ways of responding can be learned. The techniques used, in other words, must facilitate learning.

As we would expect, new attitude components are learned according to the principles of transfer, association, and need satisfaction. Many psychologists are engaged in research to determine what approaches, if any, are effective in changing attitudes through *transfer*. Information favorable to Negroes, for example, has been presented to selected groups—especially to those known to hold anti-Negro attitudes—either through the mass media, by group discussions, by formal lectures, or by person-to-person communications. Research findings so far indicate that new attitudes are more likely to be transferred through face-to-face contacts and group discussions than through impersonal lectures or mass media communications.* But the personalities of those making the personal contacts set limits on their effectiveness as agents of transfer since, as we have seen, attitudes are most easily transferred when the learner is attracted to a social "teacher" and desires to be like him. For instance, it has been found * that the more trustworthy or the more attractive the person is, the more likely will his message get through and affect existing attitudes.

Extensive use is also made of the principle of *need satisfaction* in attempts to alter attitudes. If a person comes to realize that it is to his advantage to change, the learning process may be facilitated. For example, the new ideas in a persuasive message can be presented with the endorsement of group leaders or people of high social standing. If those who receive the message are brought to realize that being accepted by others depends on their adopting a different set of attitudes, changes can come about.

A change of attitudes may also take place if appropriate conditions are made available to learn new ways of feeling and reacting through *association*. Research shows that prejudiced attitudes are markedly changed in integrated housing projects and military camps.† In these instances, Negroes have an opportunity to live among whites as social equals and to demonstrate that their behavior is not as different as most whites may believe. Although the resistance to change is usually strong, the whites may associate the presence of "good" Negroes with the familiar and pleasurable experiences of military and neighborhood life and thereby develop new and more favorable feelings and reactions to them. Feelings and reaction tendencies can also be modified, at least temporarily, by movies or TV productions that portray the everyday life and experiences of members of minority groups in such a way that a viewer can identify with the main characters and associate himself with their sorrows and happiness.

Personality and Attitude Change

Although extensive research is continuing on methods of presenting persuasive communications or creating social contexts for learning new attitudes, other research teams are focusing their attention on the personality characteristics of those whose attitudes are to be changed. As we have seen, attitudes send tenacious roots into the motivational system of the personality; any attempts to change attitudes will be limited until more is understood about the relation of attitudes to personality. And yet, the work of the late Carl Hovland and his associates at Yale and that of Leon Festinger at Stanford has already greatly advanced our understanding of this problem.

* For a review of these studies, consult D. Krech, R. S. Crutchfield and E. L. Ballachey. *Individual in society*. New York: McGraw-Hill, 1962, chapter 7.
† *Ibid.*

The Yale group * has been able to sketch out some of the personality characteristics that distinguish the highly persuasible from the nonpersuasible person. Few people, they find, react to persuasion with "discriminating flexibility," that is, being neither too susceptible nor too resistant. The few who possess this trait are sufficiently interested in their social environments to heed at least some new ideas directed their way, but are also able to distinguish and disregard what is of no relevance for them. Most people, however, vary around this ideal toward extremes. The gullible person is characterized by a marked dependence on other people and a lack of ability to critically evaluate others' propositions. This combination of traits makes him especially prone to adopt others' beliefs or any propositions that are authoritatively presented. At the other extreme, the person who is highly resistant to persuasion often lacks an ability to comprehend communicated material. He is usually negative to authority, rigid and obtuse in his thinking, and voluntarily inattentive to new ideas.

This line of investigation has been extended by William McGuire of Columbia University in his studies of the strategies people sometimes develop to "immunize" themselves against persuasion—that is, how they build up their resistance against other people's beliefs or attitudes.† As these research programs develop, we can look forward to more complete explanations of how the attitudes of *particular* people develop and change.

Milton Rosenberg ** is probing very deeply into the personality to examine attitude change. He is studying how an established system of attitude components can be broken up and then, after one component has been experimentally changed, how the system reorganizes itself. For example, what effect would a drastic change of a feeling component have on the thought-belief and reaction tendency components of an attitude? His technique is to place subjects under deep hypnosis and tamper with their feelings toward issues they value highly. To those with strong anti-Negro attitudes, he suggested that after awakening they would be "very much in favor of Negroes moving into white neighborhoods. The mere idea of Negroes moving into white neighborhoods will give you a happy, exhilarated feeling." To others who favored American aid to foreign countries, he suggested that "the mere idea of the United States giving economic aid to foreign nations will make you feel very displeased and disgusted." He also told subjects that they would be unable to remember where this idea had come from until they were given a certain signal at some later time; then they would recall that the hypnotist had planted the idea and they would revert to their original feelings. All subjects were brought out of the hypnotic state, but some were kept under the influence of the suggested change for as long as a week before the signal was finally given them.

* I. L. Janis, C. I. Hovland, and others. *Personality and persuasibility*. New Haven: Yale University Press, 1959.

† W. J. McGuire. *J. abnorm. soc. Psychol.*, 1962, 64, 241–248.

** M. Rosenberg, C. I. Hovland, W. J. McGuire, R. P. Abelson, and J. W. Brehm. *Attitude organization and change*. New Haven: Yale University Press, 1960, chapter 2.

The Social
Significance
of Attitudes

The reactions of the subjects to these "transplanted" feelings are revealing: Thoughts, beliefs, and reaction tendencies changed so as to be consistent with the new feelings; there were signs of reorganization of whole networks of related attitudes in interviews with them during the week period; and even after the original feelings were restored (as is ethically necessary in such studies) the new attitude organizations persisted to some degree, or at least the intensity of the original attitudes was reduced. Rosenberg's approach is an important new way of studying both the consistency of attitude components and their susceptibility to change.

The Desire
for Consistency and Attitude Change

[A number of social psychologists have recently turned their attention to the study of the human desire to have logically consistent attitudes. This current interest stems from the ideas of Fritz Heider * at the University of Kansas who was convinced that people seek balanced, or harmonious, relations among their attitudes and behaviors and are psychologically upset until a state of balance is achieved.] When the significance of this idea sunk in, some of the most promising theories of attitude change began to appear. First, Charles Osgood and Percy Tannenbaum † of the University of Illinois showed that people altered their attitudes when incongruities among them became obvious. For example, a person with a highly favorable attitude toward General Eisenhower and a somewhat negative attitude toward Catholicism would become less anti-Catholic if he were informed that Eisenhower was a friendly supporter of Catholicism. According to these researchers, the amount and direction of change depends on the relative intensity of the two attitudes in question: A person with a somewhat favorable attitude toward Eisenhower and a very negative attitude toward Catholicism would become less favorable to Eisenhower after receiving the same information. In this instance, no new attitude components are directly transferred; instead, the person receiving the information modifies his own attitudes to achieve a logical consistency among them.

[Leon Festinger has stimulated an extension of the same basic idea.** He argues that people have strong tendencies to resolve inconsistencies between their attitudes and their behavior.] For instance, a person who smokes may have trouble reconciling this activity with his knowledge that smoking can be unhealthy, just as the recent purchaser of a Pontiac may have trouble with his recollection that the Fords he saw and read about were about as attractive as the Pontiac. [Festinger's research has shown that people develop strategies to rid themselves of the uneasy feelings that accompany such inconsistencies. The cigarette smoker may give up cigarettes and increase the intensity of his

---

* F. Heider. *The psychology of interpersonal relations*. New York: Wiley, 1958.
† C. E. Osgood and P. H. Tannenbaum. *Psychol. Rev.*, 1955, 62, 42–55.
** L. Festinger. *A theory of cognitive dissonance*. New York: Harper & Row, 1957.

attitude toward medical research or he may keep on smoking and convince himself that medical facts about smoking are of dubious value. The Pontiac owner will likely seek out other owners of Pontiacs for support and simultaneously search for Ford owners who have had trouble with their cars.

It is apparent in these examples that a person changes his own attitudes to reduce the inconsistency between them and his behavior. Research has further demonstrated that when people are pressured into behaving in a manner inconsistent with their attitudes, attitude change is more likely to occur if the pressure is not too strong. For instance, if you were asked to make a public statement in favor of an issue you were really against, you might well experience a great deal of psychological uneasiness about the inconsistency between your ideals and your actions. But if you were well paid for doing so you would be less bothered ("Who wouldn't for that price?") than if you were simply talked into making the statement and received little in return for doing so. According to Festinger's theory, the greater the inconsistency, the stronger the need to reduce the inconsistency or psychological "dissonance." Thus, the person who received no pay for making the statement would be more prone to change his original attitude because there was a great deal of inconsistency between his ideals and his actions. The power of the theory was demonstrated in an experiment run by Festinger and J. M. Carlsmith.* They had students one by one spend an hour at a very boring task, and then asked them to tell the next student waiting to perform the same task that it was enjoyable and rather interesting. Some were paid $1, others $20 for making this false statement. As predicted, those who were paid the smaller amount changed their original attitudes about the task: By the time they were questioned later, they had apparently convinced themselves that it really wasn't too bad. For those paid $20, the task became in retrospect no less boring even though they had lied about it; they experienced much less uneasiness about their actions since they could argue, "Who wouldn't for $20?" The $1 men were upset about their actions and something had to give. It is of particular interest to us here that attitudes "give" under these conditions. We can expect that new research along these lines will greatly increase our understanding of how people change their own attitudes, particularly when these attitudes lead to annoying inconsistencies.

IN PERSPECTIVE

In this chapter we have been concerned with attitudes, defined as organized and consistent manners of thinking, feeling, and reacting with regard to people, groups, and social issues. We develop attitudes in the process of coping with our social environments and, once developed, they facilitate our adjustments by regularizing our reactions to recurring events. When they are rigidly

* L. Festinger and J. M. Carlsmith. *J. abnorm. soc. Psychol.*, 1959, 58, 203–210.

organized, however, they constrict the richness of our experiences because we tend to categorize people and events too readily into overstructured patterns of thought, and our feelings and reactions with regard to them become routinized.

Social psychologists have put a lot of work into the invention of methods of measuring attitudes. Because attitudes are not directly observable, they must be inferred either from careful observation of peoples' behavior in social situations or from patterns of responses to questionnaires that are specially designed to reflect probable modes of thinking, feeling, and reacting in actual social settings. To be of value, measures of attitudes must meet stringent standards of reliability, validity, and comprehensiveness. But the usefulness of the questionnaire technique is often limited because respondents, even when answering anonymously, become suspicious and misrepresent their thoughts and feelings. Because of this, methods are being devised that permit us to infer attitude components from behavior in experimental settings so designed that subjects are kept unaware that they are revealing cues about their real thoughts, feelings, or reaction tendencies.

Much of our social behavior is influenced by the attitudes we hold. They affect our judgments and perceptions, our efficiency in learning, our reactions to others, and even our basic philosophies of life. Ultimately, the numerous attitudes we develop come to cluster into distinctive patterns that help form the bases of our personalities.

We view attitudes as complex habits and as such we expect their development to follow principles of learning much as other types of habit do. It seems that we learn two of the components of attitudes—our feelings and reaction tendencies—through *association* and *need satisfaction*. That is, we learn to fear and avoid people and events associated with unpleasant happenings and to like and approach events associated with pleasurable happenings. We typically acquire our thoughts and beliefs (the third component) from important people in our social world who *transfer* their thoughts and beliefs to us ready-made, so to speak. Through social communication, we not only receive components of attitudes through transfer, but we also transmit our own beliefs to others.

Attempts to modify or replace attitudes rely on the same principles of learning. But it is apparently much more difficult to change or forget attitudes than it is to learn them. Because this seems to be so, we are beginning to appreciate the large role early socialization plays in attitude development.

Various strategies to modify attitudes are being investigated and compared. One promising new approach emphasizes people's normal desire to be logically consistent in their thoughts and feelings. Researchers have found that when one attitude component is experimentally modified, the others seem to undergo consistent realignment. There are even signs that people will change their own attitudes, often without being aware of it, when logical inconsistencies in their beliefs and feelings are brought to their attention.

Social Interaction

In this chapter we turn our attention to the relationships that develop among people when they come in social contact with one another. With the limited information now available, we shall attempt to explain how human associations such as friendships, cliques of acquaintances, or small groups, get established, how they develop, or, in some cases, disintegrate, and how those involved are affected by the give and take of communication. The discussion will be organized around the notion of social interaction, the process by which people influence one another through the mutual interchange of thoughts, feeling, and reac-

5

tions. Once we can recognize this process and understand some of the ways it functions, the recurring episodes that fill our daily lives take on a new significance and fascination. We begin to understand, for example, what actually takes place when two people become acquainted and in time become attracted to or dependent on each other, why a survivor suffers as he tries to adjust to the absence of interaction following the death of a loved one, why friends adjust to each other's ways of behaving, or why members of a group react against someone whose peculiar attitudes and values threaten the group's existence. We can also understand ourselves better, since none of us is ever really free from some form of social interaction. Even in our moments of solitude, we have others in our thoughts as we search for the meaning of the relationships we participate in or as we review how we acted or should have acted with others in the past and rehearse how we will behave in future social situations.

We shall examine two aspects of social interaction here. In the first section we present the learning theorist's approach to social relationships, and describe how interaction gets started, how it develops, and how those involved are affected when they receive or fail to receive satisfaction through associating with one another. Then we look at the process of interaction as a system of reactions involving two or more people, and we examine how the system functions.

SOCIAL INTERACTION
AND THE PRINCIPLE OF NEED SATISFACTION

Looked at from the point of view of the learning theorist, interaction gets underway and is maintained when both (or all) participants receive "reinforcements" for interacting—that is, when they receive something they need or want through associating with one another, the association is likely to be maintained and strengthened. Let us follow through a succession of examples of how this important principle of learning works in social relationships, starting with a case where a pigeon and an experimenter become associated with one another through interaction. Then when we proceed to examples of truly social relationships we can appreciate how the same principle of learning applies in these more complex cases.

An Experimenter and a Pigeon in Interaction

Imagine an experimenter placing a pigeon in a large, rectangular, closed-in box for the first time in its life. The particular box we have in mind is technically known as a "Skinner Box," named after Professor B. F. Skinner of Harvard who, through his ingenious research, has demonstrated the tremendous importance of reinforcements in all forms of behavior.* In its simplest form the box is empty except

* B. F. Skinner. *Science and human behavior.* New York: Macmillan, 1953.

for a coin-sized disc attached to the floor at one end. Through an opening in the top, the experimenter can watch the animal's every move. The pigeon in question has been kept hungry and wants food. The experimenter has an equally important but much more sophisticated need: He wants to control the pigeon's behavior—for instance, to have the pigeon peck the disc, not just once, but with a certain regularity. The experimenter's interest in his relationship with the pigeon is something more than that of an animal trainer: His standing as a scientist in some research center depends on his ability to bring the pigeon's actions under his control and thereby contribute to the understanding of behavior. Skinner's work has demonstrated convincingly that the animal's behavior can indeed be controlled, as we shall see. But what is of even greater interest for us at the moment is the fascinating symbiotic relationship that develops between the experimenter and pigeon as they interact.

At first, the pigeon moves nervously about the box, exploring it, attempting to get out, incidentally pecking here and there. Whenever it moves close to the disc, the experimenter rolls a kernel of corn into the box and the animal immediately eats it up. When the pigeon has received several reinforcements for being close to the disc, it tends to stay close by it and eventually, in the course of exploring, pecks the disc itself. This is a big event for the experimenter. Although he has anticipated this development, it is nevertheless an exciting experience for him to have molded the animal's behavior to this extent. It turns out to be a big event for the pigeon, too, for the moment it pecks the disc, the experimenter rolls several kernels into the box. In a surprisingly short time, the interaction is well under way: The pigeon directs itself to the disc and pecks it with increasing regularity while the experimenter carefully follows the animal's activity and reinforces each peck at the disc. Thus, the experimenter's corn-giving is under the control of the pigeon's disc-pecking, given his needs and the rules he has set up, in the same sense that the pigeon's pecking response is controlled by the reinforcements given by the experimenter.

The interaction continues as long as each participant receives reinforcements from the other. It can be stopped or modified in several ways. The pigeon could, in time, satisfy his hunger and terminate the interaction by moving away from the disc, or the experimenter could feel he has proven his point and temporarily terminate the association by taking the animal back to its cage. Furthermore, the experimenter can take the upper hand and "extinguish" the pigeon's disc-pecking by withholding reinforcements. If he does, the pigeon will gradually stop pecking the disc. Or the experimenter can modify the regularity of reinforcements and require the pigeon to peck at different rates. For example, he can get the animal to peck 20 or more times for one grain of corn if he works up to this ratio gradually. Moreover, the experimenter can make speed of pecking a requirement for reward and dole out his reinforcements only to very fast bursts. In such a case, the pigeon will peck the disc at an amazingly fast pace.

The rudimentary form of social interaction apparent in this example, then, gets underway and develops because, through their association, both participants receive reinforcements that satisfy their own particular needs. How well can this basic principle of learning account for more complex forms of interaction?

Two of a Kind in Interaction

Next we turn to the development of a relationship between two pigeons.* In this case, the experimenter is more in the background. He also has a different plan up his sleeve: to get the pigeons to cooperate. To do so, he first places one of them on each side of a small table that is divided in two by a glass partition. A row of three button-like discs has been installed on each side of the partition, in easy view from either side. The buttons are wired in pairs so that if any two adjacent discs (one on each side of the glass) are depressed at the same time, a kernel of corn automatically rolls out to each bird. The pigeons have to learn that they will be rewarded when they simultaneously peck any pair of buttons. In fact pigeons are able to learn this problem, and in doing so they learn to cooperate. At first, each explores his own compartment and buttons and when they peck a disc they are rewarded. Then the reinforcements are held off until by chance they both happen to strike adjacent discs simultaneously. When this happens both are immediately reinforced. After two or three reinforcements have been received, one pigeon tends to hover over a button on his side while the other gets set at the corresponding button on the other side. Then they peck in unison and are rewarded. The experimenter can select one particular pair of buttons (from the three possible) as the "correct" one and the birds soon learn to search it out together. Typically, one pigeon takes the lead and the other, watching attentively, follows his lead. (You might want to speculate about the outcome of interaction if two leaders were put together for the first time, or if two followers were teamed up.)

The same experiment has been carried out with young children.† The youngsters, separated by a glass partition, faced one another at a table and were told they could play as they liked with the materials they found before them. Among the playthings on both sides were a stationary metal plate in which three holes had been drilled and a metal rod. The metal parts were connected electrically so that if both children happened to stick the rods in corresponding holes simultaneously, their action would be automatically reinforced with sweets. Reward chutes delivered candies to both children if they, like the pigeons, learned to respond in unison. Although they were not even given a hint on how to play the game, once they caught on their coordinated responses increased rapidly. With the children as with the pigeons, each participant became aware of the other's importance in the sense that neither was rewarded unless they functioned as mirror images of one another. The interaction was maintained in both cases because reinforcements were made

* B. F. Skinner. *Science and human behavior,* chapter 19.
† N. H. Azrin and O. R. Lindsley. *J. abnorm. soc. Psychol.,* 1956, 52, 100–102.

contingent upon a mutual dependence of a follower on a leader and a leader on his "partner."

Parent and Infant in Interaction

Infants learn to speak through interactions with parents and other family members. Every normal infant has a complete repertoire of speech sounds at his disposal, making it possible for him to learn any language. He is, of course, encouraged to learn the particular sounds used by members of his own linguistic group: His parents reinforce his early babbling by giving him affectionate rewards in the form of smiles, caresses, even cries of delight, when his utterances come somewhat close to actual words.* Through the interaction, the child's need for affectionate attention and the parents' desire to have their child become a communicating member of the family are both satisfied. Because it is mutually satisfying, the interaction continues and the child's further attempts to reproduce appropriate words are reinforced. When the child communicates his desire for a drink of milk with a sound that vaguely resembles "milk," his attentive parents may immediately comply with his request. Signs of the infant's progress in speaking are reinforcements for the parents just as their compliance with his request is a reinforcement for the child. But the compliance not only increases the likelihood that he will learn to repeat the word, it also strengthens his tendencies to demand other things. That is, the child also learns the value of verbal interaction—through communication, he can get what he wants from others. The parents could, of course, refrain from giving the milk until he achieved a near-perfect pronunciation. By not complying immediately, they could not only increase the child's linguistic exactness, but also discourage the development of a general tendency to demand. There are two points to note here: First, social interaction between parent and child is maintained because both participants receive satisfactions through the relationship. Second, through interaction, both parties learn basic styles of reacting to others. For example, parents who are overattentive could make a "demander" of their child and the child, in turn, could make "compliers" of his parents if he showed them affection only when they yielded to his demands.

The Case of Verbal Reinforcement

Recently, it has been shown that a person can manipulate another's conversation with the appropriate use of social reinforcements. For instance, in one study college students were asked to say words that came to mind, one after another.† The experimenter led the subjects to believe that he was only interested in the progression of their ideas, whereas in actuality he was trying to direct the

---

* B. F. Skinner. *Science and human behavior,* chapter 19.
† See L. Krasner. *Psychol. Bull.,* 1958, 55, 148–170.

verbal form of their statements. He listened attentively and said "good" or "uh-*huh*" whenever a subject said a plural noun. The rate of saying plural nouns was clearly increased through the use of such verbal reinforcements as "good" or "uh-*huh*." Thus, the reinforcements helped the subjects develop certain hunches about what was expected of them in this novel social relationship so that they modified their flow of ideas in the direction desired by the experimenter.* The subjects had interpreted "good" as a form of encouragement to continue along a certain line of communication in much the same way as a person modifies his topics of conversation until his companion shows some interest. The experimenter, in this instance as with the pigeon, was reinforced by the realization that the subject was behaving according to expectations.

Other experiments have shown how effective verbal reinforcement can be in changing more complex forms of behavior. For instance, in one study, an experimenter transformed college students' normal style of forming their sentences by saying "good" whenever they happened to change, momentarily, their sentence style.† In another experiment,** college students met in individual sessions with an experimenter who asked them to talk about anything that came to mind. According to a pre-arranged plan, the experimenter said as little as possible, not even "uh-*huh*" or "is that so?" as one normally would to keep a conversation going, until the student began to talk about a particular subject matter, for example, about contemporary musicians. As the one-sided interaction started, however, the experimenter might say "uh-*huh*" if he thought the ongoing topic might in time lead to the one decided on in advance. If, for instance, the student started to discuss classical music, the experimenter would reinforce him once but participate no further until the discussion turned to modern musicians. After that, talk about musicians and reinforcements would come thick and fast. A bit later, when the discussion of the desired topic was going full steam, the experimenter would "extinguish" the student by withholding his approbation and in a short time the topic would change.

These studies indicate how actions are controlled and modified through social interaction. But in order to appreciate fully the long-term consequences of interaction, let's look beyond experiments for a moment to excerpts from a character study of a famous American author. The following description of Thomas Wolfe is that of a professional critic who very likely never heard of Professor Skinner or his notions about reinforcement. And yet in it we learn that Thomas Wolfe wrote prodigiously as though he were being reinforced for writing, much as the pigeon pecked rapidly when reinforced for doing so, and he dwelt on certain topics much as the college students did in the experiment we just examined.

* See D. Dulaney. *J. abnorm. soc. Psychol.,* 1961, 63, 251–263.

† H. Barik and W. E. Lambert. *Canad. J. Psychol.,* 1960, 14, 87–95.

** W. S. Verplanck. *J. abnorm. soc. Psychol.,* 1955, 51, 668–676.

Thomas Wolfe was a man obsessed by the act of writing. He wanted to make a complete written record of every experience he remembered, and there was never time enough for that; time was the enemy. With time at his shoulder he wrote "like a madman," "like a fiend," and "as if pursued by devils." . . . He was trying to produce a volcanic mountain of words as high as Parnassus. "It may be before I am done," he wrote . . . "that I shall say something important—that in the mad rush to get it down, something of high worth may come out."

Meanwhile he kept quoting production figures, like the manager of a busy mine from which words were being drilled and blasted like lumps of anthracite. Thus he reported in 1926: ". . . I am writing about 3,000 words a day, which I hope to increase to 4,000. . . ." In 1933: "I have written over a million words in manuscript the past four years, which makes a box five feet long by two and one-half feet wide piled to the top." The seventy-five thousand words he claimed to have written in three weeks of June, 1934—by actual count there was less than one-half as many—were the story of his father's death that appeared in *Of Time and the River,* and they were among the best words of his brief career.

He wanted to pour out everything he remembered in one torrential flood, but he also wanted to increase his reservoir of memories by going everywhere and doing everything . . . the desire to write had become "almost a crude animal appetite." *

This description of Thomas Wolfe suggests that in his early social relationships he had been so effectively reinforced for expressing himself completely that his whole personality became marked by an abnormally intense need to communicate. If the details were available, it would be fun to compare Wolfe's background and experiences in social interaction with those of William Strunk, a man who became known for his insistence of using the very minimum of words, of making "every word tell." † The point here is that a "crude animal appetite" to express everything or a tendency to make "every word tell" is very likely established through the reinforcements received over the years from others with whom we interact.

Social Interaction and Mutual Comfort

According to John Thibaut and Harold Kelley, social reinforcements account for both the continuity and the disruption of social interaction.** At the start of a relationship, each participant shows various facets of his personality, carefully observing how the other reacts to them and at the same time evaluating the recurring features of the other's personality. If the try-outs are mutually agreeable, or promise to be, interaction continues. If not, the relationship is broken. This trial period is sometimes hurried and comical, as in planned get-togethers. A good example is a freshman party at American coeducational colleges. After the newcomers are congregated, a boy typically takes a deep breath, a quick look and then dashes toward a particular girl; she has been trained to gird herself for such occasions. A brief interchange of conversation ensues during which both participants either progressively turn up the charm, or one or

* M. Cowley. The miserly millionaire of words. *The Reporter,* Feb. 7, 1957, pp. 38–40.
† W. Strunk and E. B. White. *The elements of style.* New York: Macmillan, 1959.
** J. Thibaut and H. Kelley. *The social psychology of groups.* New York: Wiley, 1959.

the other quickly turns it down, in which case the boy moves on to try again with another girl.

What is it that makes social interaction mutually agreeable in some instances and disagreeable in others? Thibaut and Kelley find that if both participants are able and willing to be helpful or friendly, or if they express similar attitudes, the relationship has promise of continuing, since both persons receive rewards through the interaction. If, however, either participant increases the other's anxiety or shows hostility to him (for example, by refusing to be helpful), the relationship is unlikely to prove viable because of the social "costs" incurred through the association. Interaction continues, then, if the rewards both participants receive from the relationship outweigh the cost involved. Associations between intimate friends provide many reciprocal rewards at low cost—that is, durable associations provide a good deal of mutual comfort.

INTERACTION AND THE THEORY OF SOCIAL SYSTEMS

Up to this point, we have given more attention to the mechanisms that get social relationships going than to the intriguing events that occur during the relationships. Our purpose in this section is to analyze these events.

If we follow the thinking of Thibaut and Kelley, we realize that people in social relationships do more than make deep psychological impressions on one another. They also become linked, through their interaction, in a coherent social "system," in the sense that their activities become interdependent so that any action of one prompts reactions and readjustments from others. When we think of interpersonal associations as social systems, we then expect the patterns of interactions between participants to be consistent and orderly and to develop systematically. For example, we would expect people who interact with one another regularly, as close friends do, to adjust to one another's ways of behaving, as elements in physical and biological systems do. Drawing other ideas from the analogy with systems, we would expect members of small groups to react against any member who threatens the existence of the group, as a physiological system reacts to changes in its equilibrium; and in general, we would expect to find a regular and orderly *change* of interaction as social relationships develop or disintegrate. Let us examine the research evidence on interaction and see whether social relationships are indeed systematic.

Mutual Adjustments in Social Systems

If social relationships are systematic, then participants in them should adjust to one another's ways of behaving. Theodore Newcomb,* a strong supporter of the theory of social

* T. M. Newcomb. *Psych. Rev.,* 1953, 60, 393–404.

systems, has suggested one important type of mutual adjustment that would be expected to take place among people who establish comfortable associations—they should adjust to one another's perceptions and attitudes, making them as similar as possible. There are good reasons why this particular form of adjustment should occur. In the first place, the more similar their perceptions and attitudes become, the more accurately participants can anticipate one another's ways of interpreting and reacting to new issues that arise. Furthermore, participants in social relationships are comforted by the feeling that their views are shared by others; because they are shared, they are believed to be socially correct. Members of a social system, then, are brought closer together psychologically if their orientations are similar, and their interaction becomes more efficient. They come to recognize the advantages of similarity: that it facilitates interaction in two-person groups and contributes to the effective functioning of larger groups. According to the theory, participants in mutually satisfying relationships should adjust their perceptions and attitudes because of the advantages derived from similarity. In other words, members of social systems are likely to establish a similarity of orientations as interaction proceeds.

What research evidence is there for such mutual adjustments of perceptions and attitudes? Joel Davitz of Yale University carried out a simple but instructive study with ten-year-olds at a summer camp.* He found that those children who chummed around together and finally became close friends by the end of the summer perceived one another as being more alike in their preferences for various camp experiences than did those who had not become close friends. In fact, close friends thought they were more alike in this respect than they actually were, for the preferences of friends were really no more similar than were those of randomly selected pairs who had not become friends. In his interpretation of the findings, Davitz argues that people have a need to be similar to others they value and like. This need, he believes, is probably developed in childhood through experiences in imitating and identifying with parents and others we care for. That is, as children we learn the instrumental value of being like people who are important to us and this value carries over into friendships as we grow older. Davitz's study points out two ways in which similarity of orientations can come about in social relationships: participants can actually modify their views so that they will be more similar, or, as Davitz found, they can be insensitive to actual differences, and think others really feel as they do. In both instances, adjustments occur that contribute to similarity, but in the latter case, where the similarities are more apparent than real, the functioning of the social system is not facilitated. What would happen in this instance if the friendships continued for a longer period of time? Would the perceptual distortions of real differences in views come to light and cause disruptions of the relationships, or would other adjustive

* J. Davitz. *J. abnorm. soc. Psychol.*, 1955, 50, 173–176.

mechanisms come into play? Newcomb's research on the acquaintance process * provides us with at least partial answers to these questions.

In Newcomb's study, 17 new men students, none of them previously acquainted, were given the opportunity to live without charge in a "student house" on a university campus, managing their own meals and making whatever living and study arrangements they wanted. In return, they were to be available an hour or so each week to members of a research team who wanted to find out what types of fellows they were and how they got along together in the house. One researcher, in fact, would live in the house as a counselor.

As the young men got to know one another, they established tentative friendships and even formed exclusive cliques. Many of the quickly formed associations, however, proved to be unstable and, during the year together, the composition of cliques changed and new friendships emerged. Through intensive interviews conducted at the start of the year and regular intervals thereafter, the researchers were able to determine: a) each man's attitudes towards various social issues, b) his perceptions of how others thought, felt, and reacted with regard to the same matters, and c) how much he liked or disliked each of the other house members. With this information, the researchers could study what roles attitudes and accurate perceptions of others played in the formation of both short-lived and longer-term friendships.

Several modes of mutual adjustment came to light in this study. As we would expect from our analysis of attitudes (Chapter 4), young men of this age would be resistant to change. Newcomb in fact found little change in basic attitudes during the year of living together. As tentative friendships were established, pairs of fellows got to know as much as possible about each other's attitudes, and then if annoying differences emerged, they would break up the budding friendship and each would develop new ones with others who actually had similar attitudes. Friendships based on actual similarities of attitudes turned out to be durable. Only in a few instances did friendships hold together because members perceived each other's attitudes to be more similar than they really were. The durable friendships were characterized by regularly increasing agreements between friends about the attractiveness of other house members. That is, friends adjusted to each other's ways of evaluating other people.

In summary, this ingenious study gives us a good look at the dynamic development of social systems. Personal desires for similarities of orientation contributed to the satisfaction and comfort derived from simple two-person friendships, and as each of the small units developed into comfortable relationships, it became easier for a number of them to function cooperatively in the house.

* T. M. Newcomb. *The acquaintance process.* New York: Holt, Rinehart and Winston, 1961.

If social relationships are systematic, then equilibrium-producing adaptations, too, should appear within the system when any one of its components causes disturbance. We have already noted what is likely to happen in two-person systems when participants are confronted with tension-producing difficulties: If mutual satisfactions cannot be obtained or if fundamental differences between participants come to light, the association usually breaks up. Here we shall examine the adjustments that take place in a small group when a member threatens the group's existence.

A particularly informative example of adaptations within a group is found in an experiment conducted by Stanley Schachter.* His purpose was to study how members of small groups react when one person expresses views completely opposed to those shared by all others. To find out, he invited college students to join newly organized campus clubs. For example, he told them that a "case-study" club was being organized at the request of local lawyers and social workers to give advice on the treatment of delinquents. Interested students could also join "editorial," "movie," or "radio" clubs, each purportedly being formed to give advice on improving the content of, respectively, magazine articles, movies, or radio programs. Schachter then organized a large number of clubs, each comprising eight or so students with common interests. Without the volunteers' knowledge, Schachter placed assistants of his in each group. One was to be consistently deviant in his expressed beliefs, and another, equally deviant at the start of the meeting, was to modify his views slowly until he was clearly in agreement with the others.

At their first meetings—in fact, there was only one meeting, after which the students were told that the whole club idea was part of an experiment—the club members were asked to decide on matters of general policy and to iron out any differences of opinion. Each case-study club, for example, to get its meeting started read through the record of a delinquent boy, and members exchanged views on how he could be helped. The deviators in each group expressed the view that the boy should be punished until he changed his ways—an opinion dramatically opposed to the consensus of the real club members.

The stage was then set to examine how the members would react to the deviators. The first development was a marked shift in communication with the two odd ones. Real club members showed a determined effort to convince them that their views were clearly inappropriate. That is, they tried to bring them back in line. This lopsided pattern of interaction became even more marked as the malleable deviator showed signs of coming along. But as it became clear near the end of the meeting that the stubborn one was a lost cause, communication with him promptly died away. By the end of the

* S. Schachter. *J. abnorm. soc. Psychol.*, 1951, 46, 190–207.

meeting he was shut out of the group and the others began closing ranks and proceeding without him. For instance, as they discussed what committees should be set up, he wasn't even considered for important positions. Also, at the end of the meeting when members were asked to indicate in private who was and who was not valuable to the group, the stubborn deviators were unanimously rejected by all groups. The main point in this experiment is that a standard procedure for managing deviance emerged spontaneously in all the groups examined. That is, orderly changes occurred in the form of group interaction, thus making it possible to counteract the disturbance of one member and insure the smooth functioning of the rest of the system.

The Orderliness of the Interaction Process,

If social relationships are systematic, then interaction should change and progress in a regular and orderly fashion as relationships develop. In this section we shall present several examples of the orderliness of interaction, along with the basic ideas of R. F. Bales and his associates at Harvard. These men have given us a comprehensive theory of social systems and have demonstrated how we can peek in at small groups as they function and observe the interaction process in operation.*

Bales looks at members of groups as actors and reactors who become related to one another through an intricate system of interaction. For him, interaction is the essential feature of groups, the mortar, so to speak, that binds people together in associations. In fact, he is convinced that the fundamental nature of any group can be explored by carefully analyzing interaction, much as an individual's personality can be fathomed by studying his free associations. If he were to eavesdrop on a private conversation or bull session among friends, or the deliberations of a formal group, he would note who had spoken to whom, who had reacted, who initiated new ideas, who kept the discussion on the track, who tried to change the topic, who generally agreed with others, who disagreed, and how frequently each person had acted or been reacted to. Rather than record the exact content of statements, he would be mainly concerned with the presumed purpose of each speaker's remarks and the effect of their statements on the course of the discussion. For instance, if, in an informal discussion among girls, one said, "I wonder how Muriel really feels about going to the dance with Bill?" Bales would record this action as a "request for opinion" of others in the group. If another replied, in an unfriendly manner, "Oh you and your questions. You're as inquisitive as Freud!" her statement would be classified as "showing antagonism." If the first girl then blushed or otherwise showed embarrassment, her emotional reaction would also be recorded. Bales would eventually slip away with a complete record of the sequence of actions and interactions among group members. With this in-

* See R. F. Bales in G. E. Swanson, T. M. Newcomb, and E. L. Hartley (eds.). *Reading in social psychology.* New York: Holt, 1952.

formation, he would make an amazingly comprehensive analysis of the group, determining how the interaction progressed from moment to moment, which members became the centers of communication, who reduced tension and who generated it, and who were likely power figures.

As part of a planned study to determine who held the power in family matters, Fred Strodtbeck, a colleague of Bales, eavesdropped on husbands and wives as they discussed their differences of opinion on certain topics.* To evoke differences, Strodtbeck first asked them to think about three families they both knew well and to give their individual opinions about which of the three had the happiest children, for example, or which was the most religious. In a good number of cases, as you might expect, the spouses disagreed and in these instances, they were asked to discuss the matter and arrive at a common decision. Strodtbeck wondered whether there would be a systematic pattern of interaction from one couple to another and whether the husband or the wife would be more likely to give in to the other in order to reach a common decision. He also wondered how a typical white Protestant American husband and wife would compare with Mormon and Navaho couples given the same questions to consider. He chose Mormons as a comparison group because in their culture women generally play a subservient role to men whereas, in the typical American family, women are believed to have equal rights with men. In Navaho culture, wives generally play more influential roles than do their husbands.

On the basis of these cultural facts, Strodtbeck predicted that the outcome of the discussions would vary in a predictable fashion from culture to culture. Observing ten couples from each cultural group, he found that American men and women won about the same number of decisions whereas the Mormon husbands and the Navaho wives were the more powerful partners in their discussions. With regard to the patterns of interaction, he found that in all three cultural groups the persons who won the decisions were the more talkative members of the pair. Furthermore, the more talkative persons tended to ask more questions, give more opinions, and show more agreement with their partners, who in turn were generally more passive, except for occasional outbursts of hostile remarks. Thus, the results indicate that the specific outcome of interaction was determined, at least in part, by the cultural background of the participants, whereas the general pattern of interaction was generally consistent from one cultural group to another.

Bales and his associates have given special attention to small discussion groups made up of six or so college students who were unacquainted with one another until called together. The researchers asked the students to discuss case studies of people facing everyday difficulties, to arrive at a consensus of opinion about the basic nature of the problem presented, and to suggest what could be done to ameliorate it. Under these conditions, it is possible to observe the development of interaction from the start of a group's existence.

* F. L. Strodtbeck, *Am. Sociol. Rev.*, 1951, 16, 468–473.

From his experience with groups of this sort, Bales believes people join formal groups with two expectations in mind. On the one hand, they expect the group to attain the goals for which it was created. That is, participants expect a seminar group to educate, a recreational group to entertain, and a conference group to sift through facts and opinions and reach generally acceptable conclusions. On the other hand, members expect to use the group setting to develop their skills in associating with others, whether they are interested in being group leaders or merely passive but well-liked participants. The social system, then, must permit the establishment of a stable status structure and an integrated set of roles that members can comfortably play. These two pressures are often antagonistic to one another, and if either is given too much emphasis, the efficiency of the system is reduced. In other words, if group members are too concerned with attaining goals or with developing pleasant interpersonal associations, they fail to satisfy one type of expectation.

From careful study of the patterns of interaction in a number of discussion groups, Bales determined how groups typically resolve this problem and ultimately satisfy both expectations.* In a remarkably systematic fashion, he found, interaction *alternates* between one person's contribution to the discussion of the case material and the emotional reactions of others to his remarks. This alternation means that attention is at one moment directed to matters of goal attainment and then to matters of interpersonal association. To illustrate, suppose one member makes a suggestion about how the discussion should turn. There are two ways of interpreting his action: first, he wants to move the discussion ahead (a goal-achievement pressure); but, second, he also wants to move it ahead according to his own plan. That is, he wants to direct the discussion, possibly in order to have others look on him as a man with particularly good ideas. The others in the group react to him and his suggestion by agreeing or disagreeing—that is, they consider the value of his idea and then rapidly decide, by what amounts to a majority vote, whether they should accept it and thereby give him status credit in the group, or whether they should compete with him by presenting their own ideas. When this decision has been made, the group has taken a step forward in establishing satisfactory role relationships and attention is then directed back to the case material again. There are two points to note here: first, that, through interaction, members become interdependent in a coherent social system, and second, that, through a regular alternation in the focus of the interaction, both types of demands of the members are satisfied, enabling the system to keep functioning as an efficient social unit.

To examine the sequence of interaction over a long period of time, Heinicke and Bales had ten groups reconvene for four separate one-hour meetings to study a different case at each meeting.† As members got accus-

---

* See R. F. Bales in G. E. Swanson, *et al. Readings in social psychology.*
† C. Heinicke and R. F. Bales. *Sociometry,* 1953, 16, 7–38.

tomed to one another, they spent less of their time in discussing the case material and more in expressing favorable or unfavorable feelings. Interpersonal communication apparently improves with experience, enabling members to accomplish more with less interaction directed specifically to the subject matter at hand. With experience, they also tolerate more disagreement and show less necessity for explicit agreement with one another's views. In fact, joking and friendly gestures replace actual specified agreements.

During the second session, however, disagreement and hostile reactions to one another's views reached their maximum, as though a conflict of some sort were coming to a head. Heinicke and Bales felt that competition for group leadership was occurring at this point. To check this after each of the four meetings they had members, in private, name the person they felt had been the best discussion leader. By the last meeting, members in four of the ten groups agreed on their leaders, whereas in six groups there were several contenders for leadership. For those groups with recognized leaders, the hostility and disagreement, so prevalent in the second meeting, clearly dissipated during the third and fourth. For the groups with several persons competing for leadership, however, the conflict continued throughout all four meetings. The sequence of interaction, then, has an orderly pattern in social systems that function smoothly, and a distinctively different, but no less orderly, pattern in systems that encounter conflict and stress.

IN PERSPECTIVE

Social interaction is the process by which people influence one another through mutual interchange of thoughts, feelings and reactions. We first examined the process from the perspective of the learning theorist, arguing that interaction gets underway and is maintained when participants receive something they need or want through associating with one another. This principle of need satisfaction seems to hold for both rudimentary forms of symbiotic relationships and more complex social interaction. Starting with the socialization process in infancy, modes of behavior and personality traits of those in social interaction are molded in part by the mutual interchange of reinforcements. Both the continuity and disruption of interaction depend on social reinforcements. Interaction continues if all participants find it agreeable; if not, relations are broken, unless their continuance is coerced.

From another point of view, people in social relationships become linked in a social "system," that is, their activities become interdependent so that one person's actions prompt reactions and adjustments from others. When the notion of social systems is examined carefully, it becomes clear from research examples that those in interaction do adjust to one another's behavior, that members of social systems do react strongly against anyone who threatens the group's existence, and that the pattern of interaction develops and changes in an orderly, systematic fashion.

Social interaction is the concern of many disciplines and it is evident from the theory and research findings now available that our current knowledge about the process and the advances that are certain to come depend on the interaction of psychologists, social psychologists, and sociologists, who have this matter as a common interest.

The Individual
in Group Settings

Let us turn our attention now to the effects of group membership on the behavior of individuals. Our purpose is to explain the psychological consequences of participation in groups, that is, to explain why some people anxiously adapt their reactions to what they think is expected of them or readily conform to group standards of behavior, while others view groups as opportunities to lead rather than follow, to set standards rather than conform to them. As we study these psychological effects of belonging to groups we shall also demonstrate, through research examples, how the behavior of individuals is affected when very

86

6

subtle changes are made in the way groups are organized. Then we shall examine how pride in one's group develops and how it can easily become exaggerated and lead to conflicts between groups, conflicts that are extremely difficult to resolve. The discussion will lead, in the final section, to the consideration of a highly personal type of conflict between groups—the conflict of allegiances commonly faced by immigrants, for example, or members of ethnic minority groups who feel unsure about their group membership, people who often wonder what groups, if any, they actually belong to.

Throughout the chapter we shall have a psychological definition of a group in mind. That is, we shall think of a group as two or more individuals who, through social interaction, depend on one another to play distinctive roles in the pursuit of common interests or goals. Thus, family groups, circles of friends, and club associates, for example, are psychological groups because they have had sufficient experience in interaction to develop expectations of how members should behave as they work for common goals. Congregations of unacquainted people, however, or mere collections of students are not psychological groups, even though it is common practice to refer to such collections as experimental groups or simply groups. In several instances we shall compare psychological groups and mere collections in terms of their impact on behavior.

The present discussion will draw on concepts already developed in previous chapters. It will become apparent, for example, that group membership affects social judgments and attitudes, and that socialization strands contribute to individual differences in reactions to groups. In particular, we shall build on our knowledge of social interaction as we study how the group affects the individual.

But still there is something special about the topic of this chapter. It has to do with awareness. While discussing interaction, we tried to bring to light various subtle processes that usually remain outside awareness. We are not normally conscious of being influenced by the social reinforcements of others or of our own use of reinforcements when dealing with others, but, as we have seen, behavior apparently does come under social control of this sort. Nor are we usually cognizant, when interacting with others, of being a member of an interdependent social system. However, we are more often aware of being influenced and regulated by other members of the groups we belong to. We know what we should not do in certain social settings and what we must do in others. When it becomes apparent to us as children that we can't explain "everything" to our parents or even to our gang, when we begin to notice the changes in our own behavior as we come to the front of a class in school to recite, when we change our styles of dress and speech because others are doing so, when we avoid being "square," then we are acknowledging social standards that set limits on our behavior. But being somewhat aware of the powerful influence of groups does not mean that we understand how groups affect our behavior. In fact, we are just beginning to understand the psychological effects of group membership because of recent advances in the theories and methods of social psychology. It is as entertaining as it is instructive to study some of these new developments.

Social Facilitation

The psychology of groups really got started about 1920 when Floyd Allport, wondering about the effect of groups on individual behavior, conducted a series of experiments on the matter.* He gave very scanty descriptions of the nature of the groups used in these studies except to say that "upperclassmen and graduate students in psychology at Harvard and Radcliff Colleges" acted as subjects, sometimes working together in small groups, and other times alone. He tested their association of ideas and the logic of their arguments, comparing the number and quality of ideas generated by those working either in groups or alone. He found that the presence of others energized individuals and speeded them up (he used the term "social facilitation") but that it cut down on the quality of their thinking. Although he concluded that work demanding concentration or original thinking would be better done in solitude, as we shall see in the discussion to follow, his conclusion and the principle of social facilitation cannot be generalized to all groups. But in spite of the limitations and vagueness of his principle, it was with research of this sort that Allport awakened the interest of psychologists and stimulated them to develop better methods of studying the behavior of individuals in various group settings. In contrast to this early course-grained approach, contemporary researchers look more carefully into both the social structure of the group in question and the personality traits of those making up the group. They also pay attention to many more aspects of behavior that may be modified in group settings. The contrast of early and contemporary approaches will become apparent below.

The Standardization of Behavior

Allport's approach may have been too general to throw much light on the psychology either of groups or of individuals. Still, many psychologists since the 1920's have attempted to give more precise, although more limited, answers to the very same problem that puzzled Allport. For example, a large number of experiments have been conducted through the years in which individuals, either alone or in group settings, were asked to make all sorts of estimates—of the lengths of lines, the sizes of rectangles, the number of beans in a bottle, the number of clicks heard, or the amount of apparent movement of a tiny spot of light in a dark room. It turns out that the judgments of individuals in group settings

* F. H. Allport. *J. exp. Psychol.,* 1920, 3, 159–182.

characteristically become more alike, tending to cluster toward an average judgment for the group. That is, those who originally deviate from the group average move in toward the average when forced to make their decisions in the presence of others. Muzafer Sherif of the University of Oklahoma argued that this movement toward an average was due to the development of a group frame of reference or "norm," that is, a group-shared standard of appropriate behavior.* For example, group members are likely to adjust their actions to the trend set by a group leader, since a leader is usually thought of as the originator of group standards or an exemplary exponent of them. In experiments on this question, Sherif noted that once the group member had moved in on an average estimate, this group norm would prevail even if the leader tried to start a new standard by changing his original estimate. The norm, then, apparently has an autonomous power and individuals regulate their behavior with reference to it.

But these demonstrations of the importance of group standards are not fully convincing because they are typically concerned with perceived estimates of the magnitude, number, or movement, of physical objects. Do group standards affect psychological functions other than perception? Would individuals' attitudes shift toward a group average when influenced by the discussion of others?

This problem was examined by Wallace Lambert and Frederick Lowy, in a study with McGill University students.† In this case, the degree of acquaintance of group members was given special attention, that is, some were psychological groups and others were groups of unacquainted students. Attitudes were measured by questionnaires administered first when the individuals were alone, then when they were in the presence of others but instructed not to talk, and a third time when they were together and free to communicate about each item of the questionnaire. Control subjects completed the questionnaire at three different times but always alone. With students who were well acquainted, it was found, attitudes clearly converged toward a group average when measured either in group settings that allowed communication or in settings where members sat next to one another but were not permitted to talk. In contrast, students who were unacquainted were unperturbed by either the presence or discussion of others. They did not change their attitudes any more than control subjects did.

These results suggest that people modify their attitudes, or at least their expression of them, if some personal advantage follows from a change. That is, the students who knew one another well probably derived benefit and comfort from the friendships. And they could doubtless estimate the acceptable range of attitudes for their group by merely noticing who was sitting with them, without any discussion. Anticipating that the attitudes they expressed would come up for discussion on some future occasion, they may have guarded against a deviance from a standard, a deviance that might threaten

* M. Sherif. *The psychology of social norms.* N.Y.: Harper, 1936.
† W. E. Lambert and F. H. Lowy. *Canad. J. Psychol.,* 1957, 11, 151–156.

their standing in the group. Students examined in the presence of others they would not be likely to meet again behaved as though there was nothing to be gained from modifying their attitudes no matter how different they might be from those of others.

Kurt Lewin was one of the first to see the implications of the effects of group standards on attitudes.* He believed that one can modify individual attitudes more effectively by changing group norms than by attempting to work directly on the individual. In this way, the acceptable range of attitudes for all members of the group could be changed in a desired direction, whereas changing one person's attitude could unduly alter his standing in his group, making him deviant in the eyes of the other members. Rather than lose his place in an important group, the individual might revert to his old attitude. It is very difficult to go it alone against a group, as we shall see in the next section.

Conformity

There has been a progressive refinement in psychological interpretations of the group's effect on the individual since the 1920's. The most recent development is a shift in interest from the notion of group standards *per se* to a more precise analysis of individual reactions to standards, that is, to the phenomenon of conformity.

Imagine that you are asked to participate in an experiment along with seven other college students. When you are all congregated in a room, a professor explains that you are to look at certain displays of straight lines and to say which of three is the shortest, calling out your answers one at a time. Suppose you happen to be sitting at an end seat around a large table and are the last to express a judgment. The first card shows three lines, one of which is clearly the shortest and all eight of you say so. On the next card, you are again sure that one line is plainly the shortest, but you hear the others, one after another, indicate another line. You don't realize that all the others are paid accomplices of the professor who have been coached to call out in a convincing manner the wrong answer for certain cards. The idea is to pressure you to conform. As they declare their judgments, your nervous smile meets serious countenances right down the line. When it's your turn, how would you react?

Judging from Solomon Asch's results with Swarthmore students,† only about 42 per cent of college students stick to their guns against the incorrect majority, and a good number go along with the majority in spite of their own certainty. In the experiment, those who did yield to the majority did so for various reasons. Asch interviewed each critical subject after the experiment. Only a very few stated that they perceived the false majority estimates as being actually correct. Most yielders saw the lines one way but be-

* M. Deutsch. Field theory in social psychology. In G. Lindzey (ed.). *Handbook of social psychology*. Cambridge: Addison-Wesley Co., 1954, Vol. 1, pp. 181–222.

† S. E. Asch. *Social psychology*. Englewood Cliffs, N.J.: Prentice-Hall, 1952.

lieved their perceptions must be incorrect. A third form of yielding was based on a fear of not appearing different. These persons disregarded what was right or wrong and paid attention only to what they should say in order to agree with the majority.

Interestingly enough, variations of this experiment established that a majority of three was as strong an influence group as was one of seven or more. Also, when a naive subject was given one other person for support against a majority of accomplices, the proportion of yielders was markedly reduced.

Richard Crutchfield of the University of California has transformed this procedure so that a number of critical subjects can be observed at one time.* In Crutchfield's set-up, individuals are seated in private booths. The tendencies to yield can be accumulated for as many as five subjects at a time, and various tasks can be demanded—judgments of lengths of lines or expressions of personal attitudes on certain issues. For example, a slide might appear on the screen in each booth showing a standard line next to several comparison lines, the problem being to decide which comparison line is the same as the standard, and to push a certain button to indicate one's choice. Another slide might present the statement "It is necessary to suspend free speech in times of crisis," the task being to indicate agreement or disagreement by pressing an appropriate key. Each person believes that he can read from a panel of lights in his own booth the answers others are giving. But in reality, the experimenter controls the sequence of lights in all booths. As in Asch's procedure, each subject is sometimes instructed to wait until the others have responded before giving his own answer, and on these critical trials he believes the others have agreed on what to him is an incorrect answer.

Because subjects are being deceived in these experiments, social psychologists usually reveal the deception as soon after the study as possible and explain the full purpose of the research. The phenomenon being studied can only be captured in a normal setting, which often requires a deception. When they are informed, subjects characteristically express respect for the methodology and the significance of the findings because they have experienced their own involvement.

Crutchfield's first study was carried out with 50 professional men, working in teams of five. From 30 to 70 per cent of them conformed to the incorrect group consensus on certain critical items. Even when attitudes were put to this test, about 30 per cent yielded to a false group consensus. For instance, to the statement "I believe we are made better by the trials and hardships of life," almost no one in the control group disagreed, whereas 31 per cent did in experimental sessions under group pressure. Even personal doubt is brought out by the technique. When asked, "I doubt whether I would make a good leader," over 30 per cent of these men, substantially more than the controls, were pressured to express their uncertainty on this personal matter.

* R. S. Crutchfield. *Amer. Psychol.*, 1955, 10, 191–198.

In another experiment Crutchfield used the technique to probe into attitudes toward socially relevant issues. He asked subjects, for example, to agree or disagree with such an item as this: "Free speech being a privilege rather than a right, it is proper for a society to suspend free speech whenever it feels itself threatened." Faced with an affirmative group consensus, 58 per cent of the critical subjects agreed in contrast to only 19 per cent of the control subjects. In this example, the social significance of the effects of group pressure becomes obvious.

Crutchfield noted large individual differences in the extent of conformity—some persons submitted 17 times out of the 21 critical trials, others yielded only once. So he examined various personality characteristics of his subjects, using well-established measures of personality traits, and correlated these with their degree of conformity. He found that the independent person, in contrast to the conformer, is more effective intellectually, is more mature, more confident, and less rigid or authoritarian. The independent and conforming persons also have decidedly different attitudes toward parents and children. The conformists tend to idealize their parents whereas the independents are more objective and realistic, both praising and criticizing. Furthermore, the conformers are more restrictive in their attitudes toward child training, the independents more permissive. It may be noted that the personality traits that characterize persons most likely to conform in social settings are very similar to those that distinguish the authoritarian person. In Chapter 4, we mentioned that the development of authoritarianism can be traced back to early childhood experiences; perhaps, as more research is completed, we shall also be able to tease out the roots of conformity.

So far we have examined what happens when people conform, but it is still not too clear *why* people conform. Edward Walker and Roger Heyns, using modifications of the basic scheme of Asch and Crutchfield, have conducted a series of intriguing studies on conformity that throw light on why people conform.* For Walker and Heyns, conformity is a way of behaving that helps a person to be accepted and liked by others. In their studies, they found that the degree of conformity depends on the attractiveness of membership in a particular group, that is, on the social rewards derived from belonging. A person will conform to norms in those groups he wants to be accepted in, and he will become a nonconformist, thereby showing his rebellion, in groups he does not find satisfying. Since most people want to be accepted in at least some groups, it follows that nearly everyone, regardless of his personality, can be made to conform when the situation is right. Because of Walker and Heyns, we can look forward to a great deal more research on the psychology of conformity in which attention will be given to both personality traits and situational factors.

* E. L. Walker and R. W. Heyns. *An anatomy for conformity.* Englewood Cliffs, N.J.: Prentice-Hall, 1962.

It is not just the social
interaction taking place in groups that affects the behavior of individuals, for people are even influenced by the passive and silent members of their groups in much the same way as an actor is affected by the mass of unknown faces that constitute his audience. In fact, one can think of social life as a series of entrances on different stages where "lines" are recited before audiences that vary in degree of expertness, of size, or of importance for the actor. A project by Seymour Wapner and Thelma Alper of Clark University tried to capture this idea, using undergraduates who were asked to "perform" before audiences of varied composition.* In one case the audience was unseen, but the students realized that people were watching and listening to them. In another, the audience—a faculty member and several students—was actually visible. In a third condition, there was no audience, except for the experimenter. The subjects' task was to select appropriate words to complete certain phrases. Hesitancy in responding was found to be greatest with the unseen audience and least with the experimenter alone. The point of the study is that people are apparently capable of behaving in various ways before others and they encounter an intellectual restraint if they have insufficient information about the audience before whom they must perform.

Why do so few persons enjoy the limelight while most of us experience some degree of stage fright? Allan Paivio of the University of Western Ontario has started an investigation of the nature of sensitivity to audiences among both adults and children.† As we noted in Chapter 2, he has been able to trace back individual differences in degree of audience anxiety in children to particular types of child-training experiences; currently he is examining how this special type of sensitivity affects performance in various social situations. As research on this problem progresses, our understanding of many aspects of the effect of a group on the behavior of an individual will be advanced.

Nonconformity and Leadership

We have seen that individuals in groups differ greatly in their reactions. Some are extremely anxious before audiences, and some are very quick to conform to group standards. Not everyone conforms to norms, however, nor does the same person conform in all the groups he is associated with. In fact, some view social groups as opportunities for setting standards rather than adjusting to them, for being themselves rather than conforming, for leading rather than following. What is it that characterizes nonconformists and group leaders?

* S. Wapner and Thelma Alper. *J. abnorm. soc. Psychol.,* 1952, 47, 222–229.
† A. Paivio, *et al. J. of Personal.,* 1959, 27, 1–17.

Social psychologists are currently considering this question from several points of view. Edward Hollander of the State University of New York, at Buffalo, for instance, believes that an individual must earn the right to be a nonconformist in his ideas and actions.* If his novel or unconventional suggestions for group action have proven valuable for other group members in the past, he is given "idiosyncrasy credits" in the group, that is, he is given the opportunity to express his ideas because others believe it is to their advantage to listen to him. If his ideas are unsuccessful, especially if they require adjustments on the part of others, he uses up his credits and is then expected to keep his ideas to himself and to listen to the proposals of others. He is expected, in other words, to let someone else try his hand at leading. A certain few are able to accumulate a large reserve of idiosyncrasy credits, thereby earning the privilege to make decisions for the group. That is, a person can earn the reputation of having good ideas and become a group leader on those grounds.

Leaders of this sort have been studied by R. F. Bales, using the techniques of analyzing social interaction that we examined in the last chapter.† He finds that they are motivated by a strong desire to control the activities of others while keeping themselves free from outside control. This role may bring them a certain type of respect, much as efficient specialists are given respect, but, according to Bales, they are unlikely to earn affection. If, instead of overplaying the specialist role, a person remains sensitive to the needs of others and helps them express their own ideas, he may gain the reputation of being the most-liked person in the group. According to Bales, it is very unlikely that one person can play both the best-idea and most-liked roles in any one group. In fact, two distinct types of leaders usually emerge in most groups. The most-liked leader appears to be motivated by strong needs for affiliation and affection.

It was this type of leader that Sigmund Freud found particularly interesting. In a fascinating little book on the psychology of groups, Freud argued that a leader emerges in a group when others find in him an object of affection.** Because they all experience a similar feeling for the leader, group members are drawn close to one another psychologically. The person striving to be most-liked, then, will be a successful leader only if he manages to keep himself at the center of the network, maintaining the bonds of affection that unite the group members.

The nature of leadership is complex. An individual may confidently strive for one type of leadership in a particular group and be a passive conformist in another. Certain settings may call out the leadership potential of many group members whereas in other contexts no one will make a bid

---

* E. P. Hollander. *Psychol. Rev.*, 1958, 65, 117–127.

† R. F. Bales in E. E. Maccoby, T. M. Newcomb, and E. L. Hartley (eds.). *Readings in social psychology.* N.Y.: Holt, 1958.

** S. Freud. *Group psychology and the analysis of the ego.* London: Hogarth Press, 1922.

to lead. These are the intriguing complexities that concern psychologists currently conducting research on the emergence of leaders in various group settings.

So far in this chapter, we have emphasized the different ways that behavior is affected by participation in groups without giving much attention to variations in group structure. Groups differ in their organization—some are formal, others informal, some autocratically structured, others democratically, some cooperatively formed, others competitively. People are clearly aware of the differences in group atmosphere associated with such organizational variations even though they may not be cognizant of how their behavior is affected by such differences. Social psychologists are currently examining how subtle changes in a group's organization can markedly affect not only the actions of individual members but also the performance of the group as a whole. This new trend is our concern in the present section.

Variations in the Form of Group Communication Networks

Social groups differ in the degree to which a member is free to communicate with others. Some are so formally structured that each person should communicate only with those immediately above or below him in the hierarchy. Others are organized around one or two people who function as a communication center that receives requests and gives out information. Still others are informal and permit free communication among all members. According to the network used, some members feel that they have central positions in the group and others feel they are in fringe positions.

Harold Leavitt of the Carnegie Institute of Technology has developed a means of examining variations in group communication networks and observing their effects on the behavior of participants.* He created an experimental analogue to various patterns of communications that commonly develop in both small groups and in large complex organizations. Leavitt limited the ways in which five-person teams could communicate while attempting to solve problems calling for the transmission of information throughout the group. Each member initially got a certain clue to the problem, but the group had to examine all five clues before the problem was solvable. For the exchange of information, each subject was required to write messages for passing on to certain others in the network. Four network patterns were

* H. J. Leavitt. *J. abnorm. soc. Psychol.,* 1951, 46, 38–50.

used: a circle, a straight line, a Y, and an X. The arrangements of the five members can be diagramed as follows:

In the circle pattern each person was permitted to communicate with those on either side of him. In the straight line, the same rule held, except that communication was limited for the two end men since they had only one other next to them. In the X pattern, the four members at the corners communicated with the man at the cross-section who in turn could pass information back to each of them. The two men on the fork points of the Y pattern could only pass information in to the man at the juncture position. Clearly with all patterns, except the circle, it is very likely that certain positions will be central and others peripheral to the flow of information. The structures also vary in their organizational flexibility. For example, the circle gives all members an equal chance to dominate whereas the X pattern virtually assures that the man at the juncture will also be the information center.

Leavitt was interested in the effect these network variations would have on the speed and efficiency of problem solving. He found that the circle and line groups were less efficient than the X and Y teams in that they used more messages to reach solutions. Yet when errors were made in the circle network, they were more easily corrected than was the case for the other patterns. Although there is inefficiency in the circle, there are more opportunities for all members to learn how to communicate, a condition that might be advantageous with subsequent problems. Furthermore, when subjects were asked how pleasant it was to participate in the experiment, those who worked in the circle pattern were the most satisfied. The feelings of satisfaction in the least structured network are believed to stem from the freedom provided by the circle's organization: The circle pattern affords (a) the most independence of action for all members, (b) the least likelihood that leaders will arise, (c) the least stability of organization, and (d) clearly the fewest feelings of being peripheral. We can expect researchers to refine this basic analogue so that the more complex aspects of group communication can be studied. We can also anticipate a great deal more attention to be directed to feelings of being central or peripheral in groups.

Unorganized and Organized Group Structures

John French was interested in comparing the behavior of individuals in unorganized and organized groups.* The unorganized "groups" he assembled were made up of college

* J. R. P. French. *J. abnorm. soc. Psychol.*, 1941, 36, 361–377.

undergraduates who were not acquainted with one another before the experiment; his organized groups were college athletic teams or established clubs from the community. He gave these groups problems to solve, some of an intellectual nature, others requiring coordinated motor performances of all members. Although the problems looked easy enough, they were chosen because they actually were very difficult or insoluble. For instance, in an intellectual problem, group members were asked to fill in rows and columns of numbers that would add across and down to a certain sum, actually an impossible problem. In a coordination problem, each member was to take one of the handles of a large cone-shaped apparatus and try, in unison, to roll a small ball up a path from the base to the top. French was interested in determining how the differently structured groups would respond to the frustration these tasks would likely generate. They were instructed to work together as teams in their attempts to complete the problems, switching from one to another if any proved difficult.

The unorganized groups, as we might expect, showed various signs of disruption and lack of interest as their attempts failed. They broke up into pairs or subgroups, working on their own, on one problem or another, or even on matters unrelated to the experiment. And yet it was the organized groups that had the greater number of minor disruptions. The members apparently were more deeply frustrated, for they directed more aggression toward one another and the demands of the experiment. Because they were among friends, they may have felt more free to express themselves than those in the unorganized groups did. Being aware that they shared a common interest in doing well as a team kept them focused on the problems as a group, but it also made them more emotionally involved. French argues that members of the organized groups were not only motivated by the demands of the experiment but also by an "own force," that is, a group-shared desire to do well as a team in anything they tried.

There were advantages and disadvantages, then, to group organization. The mutual attraction of members in organized groups sustained their motivation to succeed and kept them functioning as a team. These characteristics, of course, could be of great advantage in many circumstances. But groups that are too-well organized might suffer from a lack of flexibility in adjusting to frustration or to danger. There are two bits of information from French's work that pertain to this point. First, as we have seen, hostility and frustration seemed to spread through the organized groups more widely than through the unorganized ones. Second, in another phase of his experiment, French had members of organized and unorganized groups work in separate rooms. Later, it seemed to them that the rooms were on fire, and when they tried to get out, they found the doors firmly locked.* Of course, the smoke piped in under doors and the sounds of fire engines were all part of a rather risky experimental plan. One might expect the organized groups to attack the problem in some orderly fashion, but it was observed that fear and near

* J. R. P. French. *University of Iowa Studies in Child Welfare*, 1944, 20, 229–308.

panic spread more rapidly among the more cohesive, or organized, groups. These are only fragments of information about a highly important matter, and we must await further research to help us determine what degree of organization is most efficient for different types of groups confronting various problems. But the main point is clear: The organization of groups does make a difference in the way members behave.

Democratically
and Autocratically Structured Groups

An important investigation of the effects of variations in group structure was carried out by Kurt Lewin, Ronald Lippitt, and Ralph White at the University of Iowa.* Their interest was in creating different "social climates" for groups of 11-year-old boys by varying the manner in which the adult supervisors of the groups performed their roles. In the democratic case, the supervisor called the boys together and asked them what they would like to do with the time and resources available to them in their club house. Although he was the leader, he became a member of the group. With shirt sleeves rolled up he worked, played, and went along with agreed-upon plans as did any other member. In contrast, to create an authoritarian atmosphere, the supervisor called his group of boys together and described what they should do and how they should do it. He watched the boys carefully and told them what to do at every step in their activity.

What were the results? The authoritarian structure promoted strikingly more hostility than did the democratic organization, hostility that was usually directed to scapegoats in the group but never to the supervisor. Apathy, lack of motivation, and dependence on the supervisor became the major characteristics of the authoritarian group. The autocratic leader became the communication center, so to speak, but the communication was limited to club activities and was formal rather than spontaneous. The democratically organized groups in contrast were more free in communication. They made more statements involving the pronoun "we," gave more suggestions for policy matters, and displayed more affection for their leader. In general, these variations in leader-controlled group atmospheres had clearly and differentially affected the functioning of the whole social system. The effects were noticeable in the type of communication (which ranged from hostile to friendly), the direction of communication (among group members or toward the supervisor), and the amount of communication (from apathetic silence to a bombardment of suggestions).

* K. Lewin, R. Lippitt, and R. K. White. *J. soc. Psychol.*, 1939, 10, 271–279; R. K. White and R. Lippitt. *Autocracy and democracy.* N.Y.: Harper & Bros., 1960.

In an experiment with college students, Morton Deutsch created cooperative or competitive classroom atmospheres by subtle variations in the orientations he gave to different classes.* He told the students that instead of taking a regular course in psychology, they would meet in small seminars that would be mainly concerned with the analysis and discussion of real-life case studies. He informed the members of the competitive groups that they were to be ranked from best to worst in terms of how well they could analyze and discuss the cases and that each person's final course grade would be an average of his daily ranks. The cooperative group members heard that a large part of their course grades depended on the quality of discussion shown by the whole group. Note what these instructions mean for group members. In the cooperative setting, individual and group goals are made identical, attention is shifted away from the self to the interaction of all members, and any tendency to shine is tempered by the realization that one's contribution should move the total social system along toward the goal of effective analysis and discussion. The competitive group members, however, were set to look out for themselves since the course grade depended on their skill as individuals.

These subtle differences in instructions made a remarkable difference in performance. The cooperative groups developed into psychological groups while the competitive groups did not. Cooperative groups not only produced more ideas per unit of time but the quality of ideas was also found to be superior. The members were better able to communicate with one another, showed more integration of one another's ideas, were more friendly, and were far more satisfied with the group's performance than were the competitively organized groups. Different roles developed in the differently organized groups. For example, more members took on tasks of regulating and integrating the discussions in the cooperative case than in the competitive one, which was marked by attempts to dominate and seek personal recognition.

Deutsch's experiment demonstrates that individuals are skilled at switching their whole style of behavior, from a concern with self to concern for others, when reward is made contingent upon such a change. And once a spirit of cooperation or competition spreads, the performance of a whole group is markedly affected.

The examples of variations in group structure just presented make it evident that factors other than the personality characteristics of group members also play essential roles in influencing behavior in group settings. Behavior in groups is clearly affected by the social atmosphere created by the organization of the group. Group structures that maximize each member's

* M. Deutsch. *Hum. Relat.*, 1949, 2, 129–152 and 199–232.

The
Individual
in Group
Settings

feeling of being in the center of things, that encourage free communication, that are optimally, not overly, organized, or that generate a democratic or cooperative social climate give all members the opportunity to play distinctive and comfortable roles in the pursuit of common interests and goals. That is, the nature of the group's structure can provide the setting for the development of a psychological group in which individual differences in reactions can come into play.

THE PSYCHOLOGY OF INTERGROUP CONFLICT

People usually develop a sense of pride in the groups they belong to, a feeling that their groups are better in some respect than comparable ones they are not associated with. Whether the group pride is justified or not, group members are affected by such feelings. In certain cases it unites them and sustains them in great accomplishments. But because group pride is often developed through invidious comparisons made with similar groups one does not belong to, these feelings are potential sources of rivalry and conflict whenever groups come in contact. In fact, a good deal of the conflict we observe among neighborhood gangs, or religious groups, or nations is based on exaggerated feelings of group pride. We cannot explain such instances of intergroup conflict by merely extending our knowledge of intragroup interaction. Rather, we need information about actual social contact between groups and the effect of such contact on the behavior of group members.

A group of psychologists at the University of Oklahoma, led by Muzafer Sherif, have initiated a program of research that demonstrates how feelings of group pride develop into rivalry and conflict under certain conditions.* These investigations certainly do not answer all possible questions about intergroup conflict, but the methods and theory used to study the problem are extremely promising first steps. The researchers thought through their three-phase experimental plan very carefully. Here's how they proceeded.

They first invited 22 eleven-year-old boys from a large Oklahoma community to spend three weeks in a private summer camp. The psychologists, acting as camp directors and counselors, were able to observe the boys constantly, and to interview them at regular intervals during the three-week period. The boys were not acquainted with one another beforehand, but they had been selected because they were socially well-adjusted and intellectually bright youngsters from comfortable middle-class homes. The camp site was ideal for the realization of each phase of the experiment. For instance, it was large enough so that the 22 youngsters could be separated into two groupings, each with its own camping and athletic facilities, and far enough apart that the groups might never come in direct contact.

* M. Sherif et al. Intergroup conflict and cooperation: The Robbers Cave Experiment. University of Oklahoma Institute of Group Relations, Norman, Oklahoma, 1961; M. Sherif and Carolyn W. Sherif. Groups in harmony and tension. N.Y.: Harpers, 1953.

The first phase of the plan called for the parallel development of two distinct, cohesively organized groups. Thus, during the first week, the boys in each group decided on schedules of activities, organized athletic events, and prepared their own meals. These experiences permitted leaders, close friendships, and stable hierarchies of members to form in each group. Within a few days, group slogans, flags, and favorite songs became marks of group solidarity in both camps, and by the end of the week, two solid psychological groups had developed. According to plan, "chance" contacts between groups had occurred during the first 8 days. For example, they passed each other on hikes and the water carriers from both groups met at the spring. Within the week, members of both groups insisted on meeting the others in competitive games. This spontaneous clamor for contact, especially for competitive contact, was the sign the psychologists had been waiting for before going on to the second phase. The next step in the plan was to bring the groups together in competitive activities, encouraging the competition to develop into conflict.

The period of intergroup contact started by arranging a series of baseball games, tent-making, and tug-of-war contests—activities that would necessarily lead to victory for one group and defeat for the other. Friction between the groups became progressively apparent. Both groups resorted to derogatory slogans and hostile acts such as messing up the other group's cabin. During the second week it became clear that the time had come to turn the heat off. But the experimenters were apprehensive about the third phase because in an earlier study that also let conflict develop to a boiling point, they had not been able to resolve the hostilities completely.

The first strategy in the conflict-reduction phase was to arrange especially pleasant surroundings whenever the groups were brought together. They had the best meals of the summer in each other's presence and saw the most enjoyable movies together. But when these attempts proved to be generally ineffective in reducing the tension, the experimenters turned to another ploy. Their ingenious idea was to arrange certain situations where the cooperative efforts of all 22 boys would be required, situations, that is, that would force a merger of groups. The theory was that individuals could be diverted from their group allegiances if they could see advantages in a merger, that they would trade membership in a small group for membership in a more efficient "superordinate" group. For example, the boys were taken on a day's outing in two separate trucks, one for each group. While the boys were swimming (in separate groupings), the experimenters hid one truck in the woods and left the other in a spot between the temporary campsites of the groups; they placed a long tug-of-war rope beside the truck. When the swim was finished the boys returned to their tents, ready for lunch. The truck driver said he would go for food, but, according to plan, the truck would not start. Members of both groups watched the strained efforts of the driver as he tried to get the motor to turn over. Then one boy suggested they try to pull the truck, to get it rolling, with the rope. It was evident that it would take all the manpower available and that without the truck, no one would eat. All 22 boys joined in and after several attempts, they got the truck rolling and the motor started./ Group differences were overlooked during this task and all were visibly satisfied with their joint accomplishment. From this point on, there was a regular increase in friendly intergroup contacts, supported by a series of planned situations calling for intergroup cooperation. There were occasional relapses to separate group activities, initiated by certain fellows who felt they might lose status in a merger, but these relapses failed to catch on and became less frequent. Within three days there was convincing evidence that a new superordinate group had been formed that comfortably included the two former groups.

With this study, Sherif and his associates have not only demonstrated that intergroup conflict can be examined systematically, but they have also shown how readily people can form allegiances to their groups and how easily conflicts can develop. Their means of reducing conflict, although it has important practical implications, was a radical one because two cohesive groups were broken up in the merger. Could they have reduced the conflict and still left the groups intact? Is it possible for groups to interact harmoniously and yet maintain their separate identities? These basic problems will likely be the next steps in research on intergroup relations.

THE PSYCHOLOGICAL EFFECTS OF MULITPLE-GROUP ALLEGIANCES

All of us belong to many groups and normally we find no difficulty in adjusting our ways of behaving to fit one group or the other. Sometimes, however, we find ourselves in settings where the influences of two groups overlap and we face a conflict in adjusting to incompatible demands made on us. For instance, the boy who is dutiful and obedient in the family group but a tough and demanding leader of the neighborhood gang would be caught short if his parents should meet him by chance when he's out with the boys. Which role should he continue to play? Which group allegiance should he favor? Conflicts of this general sort are not so rare, nor so transient, for immigrants or members of cultural minority groups who, because of their special training at home and typical experiences outside, often wonder how to behave. In many cases, they are not certain which cultural group they belong to or whether they really belong to any. These conflicts are not the problems of first-generation immigrants only, nor are they easily resolved, as we shall see. Is there some way that conflicts of allegiances of this sort can be resolved? Can an individual belong to two cultural groups simultaneously, can he develop a sort of bicultural identity?

In 1943, Irving Child of Yale University, examined the dilemma of second-generation Italian young men in a New England community: Were they

Italian or American? * They had learned in childhood that they lost contact with other youngsters in their community whenever they displayed signs of their Italian background, that is, whenever they behaved as their parents had taught them to. On the other hand, if they rejected their background, they realized they could lose the many satisfactions derived from belonging to the Italian community. Child noted three typical modes of adjusting to this conflict. Some rebelled against their Italian background and made themselves as American as possible. Some rebelled the other way, rejecting American ways as much as they could while proudly associating themselves with things Italian. The third type of adjustment was an apathetic withdrawal from thinking of themselves in ethnic terms. Those who took this path tried unsuccessfully to escape the problem by avoiding situations where the matter of cultural background might come up, or by denying that there were any basic differences between Italians and Americans. In short, some tried to belong to one group or the other and some, because of strong pulls from both sides, were unable to belong to either.

Although we are introduced in this study to the difficulties faced by people who are kept on the margin of two groups, there is no evidence presented to suggest that second-generation Italians can actually feel themselves a part of both groups. In 1962, Wallace Lambert and Robert Gardner studied another ethnic minority group in New England, the French-Americans, and observed many of the same reactions as Child had noted among Italian-Americans.† But there was one important difference, as we shall see.

These researchers examined, by means of a series of attitude scales, the allegiances of French-American adolescents to both their French and American heritages. The degrees of their skill in French and English were used as a behavioral index of their mode of adjustment to the bicultural conflict they faced. In their homes, schools, and community, they had ample opportunities to learn both languages well, but whether they capitalized on the opportunities, it turned out, depended on their allegiances. Those who expressed a definite preference for the American over the French culture and who negated the value of knowing French were more proficient in English than French. They also expressed an anxiety about their progress in English. This subgroup, characterized by a general rejection of their French background, resembles in many respects the rebel reaction noted by Child. A second subgroup expressed a strong desire to be identified as French, and they showed a greater skill in French than English, especially in comprehension of French. A third group apparently faced a conflict of cultural allegiances. They were ambivalent, preferring certain features of both French and American cultures. Presumably because they had not resolved the conflict, they

* I. Child. *Italian or American? The second generation in conflict.* New Haven: Yale University Press, 1943.

† W. E. Lambert and R. C. Gardner. *A study of the roles of attitudes and motivation in second-language learning.* U.S. Office of Education, 1961 (mimeographed).

were held back in their progress in both languages when compared to the other groups. This unsuccessful mode of adjustment is strikingly similar to the apathetic reaction Child observed among certain Italian-Americans.

The fourth subgroup is of special interest. Particularly intelligent French-American young people who were unprejudiced toward foreign peoples profited from their experience with both languages and became fully bilingual. These young people had apparently surmounted the conflict and developed strategies to become members of both cultures. That is, they achieved a comfortable bicultural identity. Child had not noticed this type of adjustment in his study, perhaps because there are essential differences in the social pressures encountered by second-generation Italians and French, or perhaps because in the interval between 1943 and 1962 the heat has been turned down under the American melting pot.

These investigations reveal how important membership in groups can be for individuals, especially when they feel they have to choose between groups. The studies also highlight the importance of cultural differences, the matter we examine more carefully in the next chapter.

IN PERSPECTIVE

Our purpose in this chapter has been to explain the psychological consequences of participation in "psychological" groups, those comprised of two or more individuals who, through social interaction, depend on one another to play distinctive roles in the pursuit of common interests or goals.

Although we are vaguely aware of the powerful influence of groups, we normally do not realize how much people adapt their behavior to what they think group standards are. In examining conformity, we noted that those who design their research to determine the importance of long-term personality dispositions find support for their position as do other researchers who start with the theory that short-range influences, coming from the immediate environment, play the crucial role in determining who shall conform. Theoretical differences of this sort will undoubtedly lead to more comprehensive research on the effects of groups on individuals. But not everyone conforms to group standards. Some, it turns out, use groups as occasions to lead rather than follow, to set standards rather than adjust to them.

In pursuing our investigation of groups, we gave a good deal of attention to the ways groups may be organized and considered how very subtle changes in the structure of groups affect the behavior of those involved. Then we examined how group pride develops and how it can so easily become exaggerated and lead to stubbornly durable conflicts between groups. In the final section we considered another form of conflict between groups—the personal conflict of allegiances commonly faced by those who are unsure about their group membership, those who wonder what groups, if any, they really belong to.

Culture
and Social Psychology

In this little book we have introduced a few of the recurrent processes that social psychologists study, such as socialization, attitude development and change, judgment of social events, group formation, and communication.

These processes are caught up in, and become a part of, the great and powerful *sociocultural* processes that are the stuff of social change and that make up so much of history. Economies develop and decline, revolutions come and go, religions and values develop and change, forms of expression in the arts and sciences become flexible or freeze into outmoded dogmas, structures of so-

7

cial relationships appear to grow and divide: These are processes that occur and recur at the sociocultural level and with which we are so very much involved in the mid-twentieth century.

This leads us to the very large question we shall deal with in this chapter: What is the relation between these *sociocultural* processes and the *social-psychological* ones already considered? This, as you can well imagine, is a question to which there are probably several correct answers, and one about which there are many disagreements.

Three Answers to the Large Question

Our own answer to the large question is really three somewhat different ones for there are at least three ways in which social-psychological matters relate to sociocultural ones. Two of these we shall discuss briefly, and the third we shall entertain at greater length.

Our first answer states, humbly, that social-psychological processes are often dependent on the occurrence of the larger sociocultural processes: they are "captured"; they do not occur unless some other larger event is in progress, or has already occurred. Given a change in the law regarding integration in public schools (a sociocultural event), then there is concurrently or consequently a change in many attitudes, many new acquaintanceships are formed, the socialization of many children (and adults) is changed, new perspectives in the judgment of social events develop, new groups and new norms emerge. The occurrence of all these social-psychological processes appears to be caught up in the mainstream of the great sociocultural process of a change in the law. There is no doubt that it is often valuable to view social-psychological occurrences as caused by and captured by the widely shared events studied by sociologists and anthropologists, economists and political scientists.

This first answer—that processes like attitude change occur in a captured or dependent manner in relation to sociocultural events and processes—leads many social scientists to feel that social psychology has little to offer on larger questions. That people change their minds as the result of a new law or a new election or a revolution is interesting but of no importance causally; attitude change, for example, is merely a by-product of the great, lumbering social processes. It is merely the squeak that is made by the social machine, so to speak.

There is a second answer to our question, however. To talk of the occurrence of massive sociocultural events is often merely another and convenient way of talking about large congeries of social-psychological events. That is, the very stuff of which sociocultural events is made is often social-psychological, as when a decision to change a law rests upon the changing attitudes and social perceptions of a group of judges, and when the enforcement of a new law rests upon the slow-changing habits and values of citizens and policemen. "Diplomacy" and "politics" are often the complex interactions of persons and attitudes; economic development is a matter of changing people and of changing decisions; innovations and revolutions often *are* new social perceptions or new attitudes deriving from a very few human actors on the social scene. To believe in democracy is to recognize the threat than can come to the many from the willfulness of the few, to recognize that we must counterpoise the "majesty of the law" and "the will of the many" against the possibility that the legitimate passage of power from one group to another may be threatened by the conniving of a handful of people. Yet we also recognize the social-psychological nature of, and the human quality of, great institutions when we judge the success of a "democracy" by the degree to which it provides rights and defense to handfuls of people or even lone individuals.

Much research in social psychology is motivated by this second answer, that is, by the belief that the greater events of the sociocultural level can be understood better if they are viewed as the "macro" (or larger, summative) matters of which social psychological processes are the "micro" parts. Social psychologists bring the whole battery of scientific tools to bear on the fine texture of social and cultural events. When a social norm develops in a small group under experimental control in a social psychology laboratory, there may be a gain in knowledge that is applicable to analyzing what goes on when parliaments debate, cabinets decide, union locals vote, or individuals go to the polls. There *may* be such a gain: It is not yet certain, and it is only when we try out our micro knowledge on the actual macro events that we can check out the value of social psychology for the study of larger social issues.

Which brings us to a third answer to our large question: Social-psychological processes are causally important as events that *mediate* or *integrate* the broadly shared events and processes occurring in society and culture, regardless of whether or not society and culture are made of social-psychological stuff. From this position we can view the relationship of the sociocultural and the social-psychological as in this example: Given that the Volstead Act is passed by the United States Congress (a sociocultural event that may have resulted from a set of sociocultural processes), it is vital to the success of that act that a great many people change their attitudes toward the drinking of whiskey. If the attitudes (and social habits) change toward a dropping of the habit, then the law can be enforced (which is another sociocultural process); if not, enforcement cannot follow. In this historic example, the social-psychological events did *not* follow the new law, and enforcement therefore, did *not* and, could not presumably, follow without enormous cost. To come closer to the present: Unless some deep-seated attitudes and habits change as a result of the Supreme Court decision to outlaw segregation in American schools, then the enforcement of the decision will be slowed or defeated. The change of attitudes and habits is causally vital in this (and probably all) social change: Its occurrence or nonoccurrence permits or halts the larger social process.

This third answer to the large question seems the most satisfactory because it recognizes much of the wisdom in the other answers, though it does rule out the notion that social-psychological processes are *always* by-products of social processes. It recognizes too that social-psychological processes are often captured, caught up in, or caused, by sociocultural ones; it further recognizes that social-psychological matters may in their turn be causally linked to sociocultural ones, serving to mediate or to integrate aspects of the larger social world.

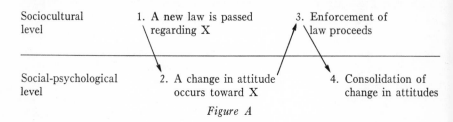

Figure A

Figure A provides a simple, anecdotal example of what we are talking about. The scientific imagination can be put to work here, and various levels of down-up or even up-down combinations may be developed and the resultant hypotheses may be put to test by systematically collecting information on large numbers of cases. We must sometimes visualize a *number* of steps at one or both of the levels in order to cast light systematically on issues of great moment.

Most of the truly systematic work on this problem of relating social psychology to the events of the larger society has involved the analysis of *past* cases. This is a sensible starting point for evaluating the usefulness of some of our social-psychological principles, but we are now beginning to move to the more positive task of predicting *future* changes in societies or in social-psychological and psychological processes and events.

Let us look at some recent research attempts, and then return to consider the chicken-or-egg nature of causal analysis. The important aim is to discover useful systematic order, not necessarily to deal with historical ultimate causes.

PERSONALITY AND ECONOMIC DEVELOPMENT

David McClelland,* a Harvard social psychologist whose work on achievement motivation was discussed in the second chapter, has extended his search to the sociocultural realm. He argues that the process of *economic development* of a country is in part a social-psychological matter since it is highly

* See David McClelland. *The achieving society*. Princeton: D. Van Nostrand Co., 1961.

correlated with early independence training and with the resultant presence of high need for achievement in a sufficient number of the people in the country concerned. The society can then take off into greater economic development, other things equal. We can simplify some of McClelland's ideas as follows:

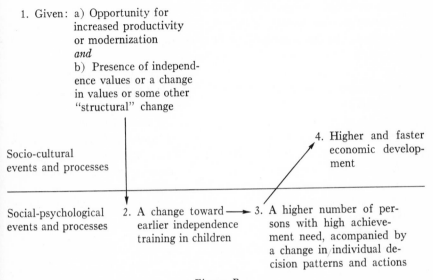

1. Given: a) Opportunity for increased productivity or modernization *and* b) Presence of independence values or a change in values or some other "structural" change

Socio-cultural events and processes

4. Higher and faster economic development

Social-psychological events and processes

2. A change toward earlier independence training in children

3. A higher number of persons with high achievement need, acompanied by a change in individual decision patterns and actions

Figure B

Let us note at once that McClelland is not saying that the social-psychological factors can operate alone to solve the problem of economic development. Economic opportunity and aid are also necessary. The point is that development often *fails* to occur or to be consolidated because the socio-cultural conditions that favor the development of achievement motivation are not present. Development *does* tend to occur when these conditions *are* present, that is, when the presence of the correct *shared* values, or a change in values, or a structural change in the educational systems occurs which in turn sets off the processes *below* the line in Figure B. Then parents and teachers move toward emphasis on earlier independence training in their formal and informal relations with children. This creates greater need for achievement in a larger number of children. This, in turn, results in a higher level of trying to do well when excellence of performance is an issue, when the measure of excellence is clear, and where some medium level of risk is involved. It is people with these values who make government efficient and business hum.

McClelland's is a bold argument that gives social-psychological factors a central place in an important area of human affairs, and McClelland presents many kinds of research findings, most of which are consistent with his causal argument. Each of the arrows in Figure B has been investigated, in at least an indirect way.

The first arrow has usually been approached by studying the already existing value systems, religious or otherwise, of various subgroups in America or Europe and relating them to child-training practices or the resultant strength of the need for achievement. The second arrow has been studied by relating the history of a child's independence training to the strength of his achievement motivation, as we outlined in Chapter 2. McClelland has also checked the implications of this hypothesis by showing that if in a simple society the parents tend to emphasize early mastery and self-reliance in a child, then the myths or stories of the society will be more filled with themes relating to achievement than if early independence training is not emphasized.

You should note the strategy of proof here: McClelland is providing a systematic array of evidence of many kinds that agrees with or *converges* on the implications of the theory, rather than resting on any one study for his proof. He does so for two reasons: It is exceedingly difficult or downright impossible to experimentally alter societies in ways that would test his theory. Further, his hypothesis is very broad and inclusive, holding, he feels, for all periods of history and all countries.

It is therefore sensible to test for *what would be expected to hold if the theory were correct* in the past history of great nations that have risen economically, fallen, and even risen again and again. He has done so ingeniously and in an increasingly persuasive manner. It is possible, for example, to count the occurrence of achievement themes in the orations read at the funerals of ancient Greeks; we can view such a count as a measure of 1 (or alternatively of 3) in Figure B. It is possible to measure 4 in the figure, at least indirectly, by noting the changes over the years in the distance from Athens that Greek vases were found, the fluctuations betokening the expansion and contraction of the Greek trading activities. When these two, the measures of achievement motivations and of economic expansion, are related to one another over time, the interesting pattern emerges that the maximal rise in economic expansion occurs several generations *after* the achievement imagery has been at its height, and the decline in economic expansion occurs sometime *after* the achievement imagery has fallen. The economic growth and decline, then, is possibly caused by the changes in character of the people as reflected in what is valued in the funeral orations of the time. The decline, McClelland suggests, may have been occasioned by an increase in the use of slaves to rear children during the wealthy period. This may have led to less pressure in child training toward early independence training and thus to a decline in achievement motivation in the more pampered children.

Although McClelland has done similar studies on most of the other great empires of history, his most practical findings come from modern times. In studying the relationship between 1 and 2 in Figure B, he shows that in the United States or in Europe the people who hold religious values close to what sociologists refer to as the "Protestant Ethic" (which involves a complex of beliefs, including those in a personal relationship to the Deity, self-advancement and self-perfection) tend to push their children toward early independence training. But most vital of all, he shows that if a country fills the school reading material of children with signs of achievement striving (an indirect measure of the parental practices with regard to training children), then *in the next generation* there will be a greater increase in the economic level of productivity in the country.

McClelland leans heavily on his argument here: The need achievement in children's readers in 1950 cannot be predicted from the economic position of the country in 1925, yet it is possible to predict economic growth (as of 1950) from the need achievement in children's readers in 1925. It is even possible to predict somewhat the economic growth from 1950 to 1958 from similar (1950) measures of children's readers in a manner that cannot be predicted from strictly economic data. This argument is indirect in that the measure of achievement motivation is not taken from children themselves nor is it taken directly from the child-training practices that McClelland believes must precede high personal achievement motivation. Indirect or not, however, it is impressive evidence that social-psychological matters (the motivational basis of imagery contained in reading matter) is interwoven in a consistent way with a sociocultural economic process that is so much an issue in the modern world. These findings are also consistent with—even if they do not crucially prove—the kind of causal sequence outlined in Figure B. Crucial proof of causal relations in this realm of culture and personality are frequently sought but rarely achieved. McClelland's work, however, has the great value of suggesting, for example, that if a society wishes to add to its economic wealth it should look (among other places) to its human resources in terms of deep and early motivations and it should reorder its family life along with increasing its economic opportunities. In short, cultural change and social-psychological processes may often be causally linked in the up-and-down, down-and-up fashion of Figure **B**.

PERSONALITY AND EXPRESSIVE CULTURAL MODELS

Human games and pastimes have fascinated both anthropologists and social psychologists for a long time. And well they should, because the games of a people are part of their culture and general style of life yet at the same time they attract a good deal of individual, spontaneous involvement. The careful study of games should therefore provide insights into both the people and their culture, and some of these insights have begun to emerge from the systematic collaborative work of John Roberts, an anthropologist, and Brian Sutton-Smith, a psychologist.*

These researchers believe that games *model* important aspects of culture

* See John M. Roberts and Brian Sutton-Smith. *Ethnology,* Vol. I, No. 2, 1962.

and at the same time serve to *express* the needs of the people who choose to play them. Games are therefore an important case of a larger class of *expressive models*, as, in an even more removed sense, are folk tales. Games also have two functions besides that of providing a refreshing way to ward off boredom: They provide a way of teaching people in a society (particularly the young) some ways of getting important things done; they also provide a kind of therapy, in that individuals who are in conflict about getting their actual cultural work done can live for a time in an easier fantasy world of expressive models and evade the world of those things which are modelled until their feeling of conflict passes.

Roberts and Sutton-Smith offer exciting insights when they get specific about just what games teach people and just what feelings of conflict can be assuaged by what games. Both of these questions demand a classification of games, and this Roberts has provided. He finds that there are three important kinds of games, each modelling different sorts of activities and providing the players an opportunity to practice *different styles,* or *attitudes,* toward competition: 1) games of *physical* skill, such as a footrace, model cultural activities like chasing a runaway sheep and permit rehearsal of the attitude of hope for success by the exercise of speed and power; 2) games of *strategy,* such as poker or Monopoly, model the activities of the market place and provide rehearsal of the attitude of hope for success by the exercise of clever decision-making; 3) games of *chance,* like roulette, reflect activities like striking it rich in the gold fields, and provide practice in the hope for success by luck. Examples of folk tales that preponderantly involve these same classes of expressive models are 1) the tortoise and the hare for physical skill, 2) the fisherman and his wife for strategy, and 3) the story of Cinderella for chance.

We can schematize the causal assumptions of Roberts and Sutton-Smith by another diagram relating the sociocultural level to the social-psychological one, as in Figure C:

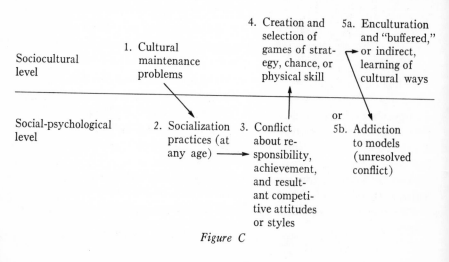

Figure C

As in the case of McClelland's theory, it is quite difficult to test the theory of Figure C crucially and directly, so Roberts and Sutton-Smith have systematically tested the implications of each of the arrows of the figure. Let us look at a few of their tests.

One of the first tests had to do with the general relationship between 1 and 4 in the diagram. The hypothesis was that the games actually played in a culture would model some aspect of the maintenance problems of the society as a whole. The findings were consistent. Games of strategy exist in complex primitive societies but they tend to be absent in simple primitive societies that lack political integration and social classes. This difference suggests that games of strategy are related to problems of controlling complex social systems. Games of chance are related to the supernatural cultural systems, so they tend to be absent in societies that view gods and spirits as mainly malevolent, but are present where supernatural beings are believed to be benevolent more than half the time. Games of physical skill, in turn, are related to a complex of environmental factors, being present, for example, in greater numbers in temperate climates but absent in the tropics.

But the theory demonstrated in Figure C suggests that the selection or creation of games at the sociocultural level is causally *mediated* by the presence or absence of certain psychological conflicts that arise from socialization practices. Here Roberts and Sutton-Smith are able to test the indirect implications of the theory both cross-culturally (where total societies are the unit of analysis) and intra-culturally (where individuals or sex groupings are the unit of analysis). The cogency of their theory is strengthened by these findings both within and across cultures relating 3 and 4 in the Figure: 1) the selection of (or creation of) strategy games is linked with pressure for (and probably conflict over) *obedience* in socialization; 2) chance games are associated with *responsibility* training; and 3) physical skill games crop up or are preferred where *achievement* pressures are high. Cross-culturally speaking, it is also interesting that where there is a wide array of *kinds* of games in a society there is strong anxiety over achievement performance. In short, in a "game culture" the several kinds of games provide an opportunity for individuals to assuage anxiety engendered by their conflict over achievement behavior (because winning or losing in the game has no actual collateral outcome), while at the same time rehearsing the players in the very processes of competition themselves.

We can only touch on the rich findings that have been collected around the theory of Figure C. Roberts and Sutton-Smith report, for example, on a study of preference for games of a large number of American boys as compared to girls. There is considerable evidence from both cross-cultural and American sources that boys are given higher achievement training whereas girls are given more consistent obedience and responsibility training. Consistent with this assertion, American girls show a greater preference for games of strategy (like I've Got a Secret or Twenty Questions) and for games of chance (like Bingo, Spin-the-Bottle, or Post Office), while the boys prefer games of pure physical skill (like bowling, horseshoes, racing) or games that involve both physical skill and strategy (marbles, wrestling).

The final set of arrows in Figure C have to do with the *effects* on people of playing games. There can be the (usual) effect of teaching the players something about the activities and rules of the society under conditions of "buffered," or reduced, intellectual and emotional scale (5a), or it can have the effect of leaving some of the players addicted to the games they play, presumably due to the particularly strong psychological conflicts they entered the game with (5b). Work on this last aspect of the theory has only begun, but preliminary work points up the probability that college students who are addicted to such games of strategy as poker, even to the point of playing the game as much as 40 hours a week, are laboring under a particularly strong set of conflicts about their positions in the social system.

This theory of games has many practical ramifications, many of them as yet unstudied. There is enough evidence to suggest, however, that a theory that joins the sociocultural and social-psychological realms in the down-up-down fashion of Figure C is a fruitful way of thinking about the relationship of social psychology to large-scale cultural and sociological matters.

OTHER SOURCES OF PERSONALITY AND CULTURE

Our discussion of the relation of social psychology to economic development and to cultural models, brief though it be, does introduce some of the causal complexities that arise from the large question we asked at the opening of this chapter. You should not be led to feel, however, that all behavioral scientists think in the down-up-down-up interdisciplinary fashion we have emphasized here. Many factors in the determination of social behavior are still profitably studied in a single-level or single-discipline manner. It may always be profitable to study social-phychological processes at their own level, as most of this book attests.

Nor should you be led to think that the work of Roberts and McClelland covers all the possible sources of personality or of culture. In order to dispel any such illusion let us look briefly at two studies that show the probable importance of 1) *climate* as a source of culture and personality, and 2) religious beliefs as causes of personality training.

John W. M. Whiting,* a Harvard behavioral scientist who has been very influential in this area, has shown with cross-cultural evidence that the cultural practice of circumcision rites for boys is related to, and possibly causally involved with, the cultural occurrence of a) exclusive mother-infant sleeping arrangements (where the child sleeps with the mother for several years until another baby or the father turn him out), b) a long *post-partum* sex

* J. W. M. Whiting. Effects of climate upon certain cultural practices. *Lab. of Human Dev.*, Harvard University, 1963. (In Ward Goodenough, ed., *Explorations in Cultural Anthropology,* New York: McGraw-Hill, in press.)

taboo (in which sexual intercourse between parents is forbidden for some time following birth of a child), and c) patrilocal residence (a cultural pattern in which a newly married couple live in the vicinity of the *man's* family). Whiting has emphasized the possibility that the circumcision rites for boys are possibly a means to break the strong emotional bond of identification of the boys with their mothers, which developed in the long period of exclusive attention received by the boys.

Whiting has recently analyzed his findings more fully. He shows empirically that patrilocal residence tends to be found where polygyny is practiced, and it is in these polygynous societies that the prolonged *post-partum* sex taboo is found. In turn, the sex taboo is related—and to Whiting, anchored causally—to protein deficiency in the diet of the region (which is usually in the rainy tropical climates of the world). Where mother's milk is the main source of protein for the infant, the mother must avoid becoming pregnant so that her milk will remain rich in protein. The sex taboo, therefore, has developed to help the newborn child avoid the protein deficiency disease, called *Kwashiorkor,* which is so tragically prevalent in these hot and humid areas.

The causal sequence, then, goes like this: Given low protein diet, a long sex taboo after birth arises to ward off the effects of the dietary deficiencies. This taboo leads men to look for other women, thence polygyny arises, thus keeping the husband's new sexual relation "in the family," and this polygyny leads to the patrilocal residence pattern because the husband's relatives who surround the co-wives help to keep them in line.

Finally, Whiting shows empirically that the exclusive mother-child sleeping arrangments tend to occur where the mild winter temperatures (and hot summer ones) lead husbands and wives to sleep apart. It would appear, then, that a number of these basic cultural phenomena—sex taboos, residence patterns, sleeping arrangements, polygyny, and even circumcision rites—may all turn out to be, in part at least, clearly determined adjustments to some basic climatic and dietary facts of life.

In vast contrast to climate factors lies the realm of ideas, and one must not underestimate the power of ideas as causes both of personality and culture. An example can be found in a study by William Lambert, Leigh Triandis, and Margery Wolf * on the correlates of beliefs in simple societies that supernatural beings are benevolent or malevolent. The study shows that in societies that conceive of the deities as being preponderantly malevolent— causing trouble, calamities, illness, and death—most of these cultural religious beliefs can be sensibly viewed as *reflections* of the usual treatment received by a member of the societies during early socialization. For example, the infants in these societies receive more painful experiences at the hands of their otherwise affectionate parents than do children in societies where the deities

* W. W. Lambert, L. M. Triandis, and M. Wolf. *J. abnorm. soc. Psychol.,* Vol. 58, No. 2, March, 1959.

are seen as preponderantly kind, and parents in such societies generally make a great use of punishment in rearing children.

One aspect of the story is not easy to understand, however. These usually punishing parents go out of their way to reward their children positively for self-reliant and independent behavior. The simplest explanation of the paradox appears to be that, imbued as they are with the notion that the world is a trap in which even the supernaturals are malevolent, these parents go out of their way to reward their children for behaving in just those self-reliant and independent ways that would prepare them for surviving in a tough world.

In short, the experiences in infancy of pain and punishment seem to explain why both the parents and the new child would come to have expectations of harm from the powerful deities, but we can best explain the parents' behavior in rewarding self-reliance and independence as being due to their religious *belief* about the supernatural. No apparent outstanding climatic or geographical features can explain the value placed on these behaviors in children. Infant socialization practices color the religious beliefs, the religious beliefs in turn determine some of the child-training practices, and this cultural pattern helps determine personality. So goes the interpretation.

IN PERSPECTIVE

This interpretation, with all its circular form, may well symbolize for us the circularity of a good many of the causal sequences in the relations between social-psychological processes and those of the broader culture and society. Our aim in social psychology, as well as in the greater issues of behavioral science, is to study the facts of social life with systematic diligence and with the greatest rigor available. We will continue to question the causal explanations in this realm as long as we continue to delight in this restless quest that has given us a modern social psychology.

The restlessness is not new. Both the circular nature of many of the *causal* processes in the realm of culture and personality and the circular nature of the *practical use* of our knowledge about these processes is captured in this restless but hopeful passage, written by Confucius around 500 B.C.:

The ancients who wished to illustrate the highest virtue throughout the empire first ordered well their own states. Wishing to order well their states, they first regulated their families. Wishing to regulate their families, they first cultivated their own selves. Wishing to cultivate their own selves they first rectified their hearts. Wishing to rectify their hearts, they first sought to be sincere in their thoughts. Wishing to be sincere in their thoughts, they first extended to the utmost their knowledge. Such extension of knowledge lay in the investigation of things.

Things being investigated, knowledge became complete. Their knowledge being complete, their thoughts were sincere. Their thoughts being sincere, their hearts were then rectified. Their hearts being rectified, their own selves were cultivated. Their own selves being cultivated, their families were regulated. Their families being regulated, their states were rightly governed. Their states being rightly governed, the whole empire was made tranquil and happy.

Selected Readings

Chapter 1

Allport, G. W. The historical background of modern social psychology. In G. Lindzey (Ed.). *Handbook of social psychology.* Vol. 1. Cambridge: Addison-Wesley, 1954.

Hollander, E. P. and R. G. Hunt. *Current perspectives in social psychology.* New York: Oxford, 1963.

Chapter 2

Child, I. Socialization. In G. Lindzey (Ed.). *Handbook of social psychology.* Vol. 2. Cambridge: Addison-Wesley, 1954.

Sears, R. R., E. E. Maccoby, and H. Levin. *Patterns of child rearing.* New York: Harper & Row, 1957.

Whiting, B. (Ed.). *Six cultures: studies of child rearing.* New York: Wiley, 1963.

Chapter 3

Hochberg, J. E. *Perception.* Englewood Cliffs, N. J.: Prentice-Hall, 1964.

Maccoby, E. E., T. Newcomb, and E. L. Hartley. *Readings in social psychology* (3rd. ed.). New York: Holt, Rinehart and Winston, 1958.

Chapter 4

Brown, R. *Models of attitude change.* In R. Brown, *et al. New directions in psychology.* New York: Holt, Rinehart and Winston, 1962.

Campbell, D. Social attitudes and other behavioral dispositions. In S. Koch (Ed.). *Psychology, a study of a science.* Vol. 6. New York: McGraw-Hill, 1963.

Edwards, A. L. *Techniques of attitude scale construction.* New York: Appleton-Century-Crofts, 1957.

Klineberg, O. *Social psychology.* New York: Holt, Rinehart and Winston, 1954.

Osgood, C. E., G. J. Suci, and P. H. Tannenbaum. *The measurement of meaning.* Urbana: University of Illinois Press, 1957.

Rosenberg, M. J., C. I. Hovland, W. J. McGuire, R. P. Abelson, and J. W. Brehm. *Attitude organization and change.* New Haven: Yale University Press, 1960.

Chapter 5

Heider, F. *The psychology of interpersonal relations.* New York: Wiley, 1958.

Homans, G. C. *The human group.* New York: Harcourt, Brace & World, 1950.

Newcomb, T. M. *The acquaintance process.* New York: Holt, Rinehart and Winston, 1961.

Skinner, B. F. *Science and human behavior.* New York: Macmillan, 1953.

Thibaut, J., and H. Kelley. *The social psychology of groups.* New York: Wiley, 1959.

Chapter 6

Asch, S. E. *Social psychology.* Englewood Cliffs, N. J.: Prentice-Hall, 1952.

Sherif, M., *et al. Intergroup conflict and cooperation: The Robbers Cave Experiment.* Norman, Oklahoma: Institute of Group Relations, 1961.

Walker, E. L. and R. W. Heyns. *An anatomy for conformity.* Englewood Cliffs, N. J.: Prentice-Hall, 1962.

White, R. K. and R. Lippitt. *Autocracy and democracy.* New York: Harper & Row, 1960.

Chapter 7

McClelland, D. C. *The achieving society.* Princeton: D. Van Nostrand, 1961.

Triandis, L. M., W. W. Lambert, *et al. Mothers of six cultures.* New York: Wiley, 1964.

Whiting, J. W. M. and I. Child. *Child training and personality.* New Haven: Yale University Press, 1954.

Index

Machiavellianism, 33
Majority, perception of, 42–43
Masculine role, 21
Mead, George Herbert, 44
Miller, Neal E., 19
Minority groups, 56, 60, 102–104
Mowrer, O. Hobart, 23

N

Newcomb, Theodore M., 2, 63, 77, 79, 81n, 94n

O

Occupations, attitude toward, 47
Oedipus complex, 15
Organization of groups (see Groups)
Orleans, S., 13n
Osgood, Charles, 17, 67n

P

Pain tolerance and social attitudes, 56–57
Paivio, Allan, 23, 93
Participation (see Group participation)
Perception, 30: and action, 30–31; of contributions in a group, 41–42; of facial expression, 33–34; failures of, 29–30; of hierarchies, 40–41; of others' intentions, 37–38; of a majority, 42–43; of line of regard, 32–33; of others' personalities, 34–36; of role, 45–47; of social causality, 38–40; and social concepts, 43; of social events, 29, 31, 36
Personality formation: and economic development, 108–111; and the family, 12–13; and games, 111–114; and social settings, 11–12
Persuasion, 38–39
Pigeons in social interaction, 71–73
Polygyny, 115
Poser, E. G., 55n
Prejudice (see also Attitudes): development of, 49–50, 62–63; effect on social perception, 47; and learning, 57–59, 64, 65; measurement of, 52–54; and personality, 60–61
Preston, A., 13n
"Protestant ethic," 111

R

Rabson, A., 13n
Race, attitude toward, 47
Reinforcement, 71–76
Religion, attitude toward, 47
Religious beliefs and socialization, 115–116
Resocialization, 8–10
Riecken, Henry, 38, 41–42
Roberts, John, 111–113
Roles, 20–22, 45–47
Rommetveit, Ragnar, 44–45, 46
Rosen, Bernard, 26
Rosenberg, Milton, 66
Rosenblith, Judy F., 63n

S

Schachter, Stanley, 24–25, 80
Schein, Edgar, 9
Schlosberg, Harold, 34
Sears, Robert R., 17, 23

Segregation, in schools, 107
Self-consciousness, 23–24
Sherif, Carolyn W., 100n
Sherif, Muzafer, 89, 100
Skinner, B. F., 71, 73n, 74n, 75
Social concepts, developing, 44–45
"Social distance scale," 52
Social hierarchies, 40–41
Social interaction (see Interaction)
Social perception (see Perception)
Social psychology: definition, 1; and economic development, 108–111; methods of research in, 3–5; as a scientific discipline, 1–5; and sociocultural processes, 106–108
Social roles (see Roles)
Social settings, 11–13
Social systems: disturbances in, 80–81; mutual adjustment in, 77–79
Socialization: of achievement needs, 26–27; of aggressiveness, 15–18; and birth order, 24–25; of conscience, 22–23; by identification, 20–22; by imitation, 18–19; role of community, 10–12; role of family, 12–13; resocialization, 8–9; of social compliance, 13–15; of stage fright, 23–24; vicarious, 19–20
Sociocultural processes, 105: personality and economic development, 108–111; and social-psychological processes, 106–108; theory of games, 111–114
Stage fright, 23–24
Status and perception, 38–39
Stevenson, M., 21n
Strauss, A., 44n
Strickland, Lloyd, 39
Strodtbeck, Fred, L., 82
Strunk, William, 76
Sutton-Smith, Brian, 111–113
Swanson, G. E., 81n, 83n

T

Tagiuri, Renato, 39
Tannenbaum, P. H., 67
Thematic Apperception Test, 26
Thibaut, John, 38, 76
Triandis, Harry, 34, 46
Triandis, Leigh, 116

V

Verplanck, W. S., 75n
Volstead Act, 107

W

Walker, Edward L., 92
Wapner, Seymour, 93
White, E. B., 76n
White, Ralph, 98
Whiting, B., 12n
Whiting, John M. W., 21, 114
Winterbottom, Marian R., 26
Wishner, Julius, 35
Wolf, A., 34n
Wolf, Margery, 116
Wolfe, Thomas, 75–76
Woodworth, Robert, 34
World War II, effect on children, 21
Wright, Herbert F., 11